Praise for
What's Really Holding You Back?

"Valorie helps us discover and evaluate the issues and challenges that hold us back and keep us from becoming all we were created to be. Jesus said He came that we might have life and have it abundantly. This book will supply you with the answers that will help you move into an abundant, fulfilling future."

—TERRY MEEUWSEN, co-host of *The 700 Club*

"Everybody can use a little help getting out of a rut, and this book by Valorie Burton is just the boost you need. Whether you're having trouble reaching a major goal in life or you just want to stay on top of your game, Valorie has some inspiring words that will take you to the next level."

—TOM JOYNER, syndicated radio personality

"With the skill of a surgeon, Valorie Burton uses her scalpel to dissect our lives into the major issues that hold us back, and then she provides us with the practical prescription for a breakthrough in each area. If you could use a breakthrough, you will love this book!"

—BILL BUTTERWORTH, author of *The Promise of the Second Wind* and *New Life After Divorce*

"If anything is in the way of your success and happiness, this book will help you remove those barriers. Valorie Burton gives readers the insight, tools, and motivation needed to lead a healthier, wealthier, and wiser lifestyle."

—EDWIN V. AVENT, publisher of *Heart and Soul* magazine

"Valorie Burton offers a refreshing approach to tackling those obstacles—real or imagined—that hold you back from enjoying a spectacular life."

—MONIQUE GREENWOOD, owner of Akwaaba Bed & Breakfast Inns and author of *Having What Matters: The Black Woman's Guide to Creating the Life You Really Want*

What's Really Holding You Back

Closing the Gap

Between

Where You Are

and Where

You Want to Be

Valorie Burton

Jonah — Persevere!

Valorie B

WATERBROOK
PRESS

WHAT'S *REALLY* HOLDING YOU BACK?
PUBLISHED BY WATERBROOK PRESS
12265 Oracle Boulevard, Suite 200
Colorado Springs, Colorado 80921

All Scripture quotations, unless otherwise indicated, are taken from the *New King James Version*. Copyright © 1982 by Thomas Nelson, Inc. Used by permission. All rights reserved. Scripture quotations marked (NIV) are taken from the *Holy Bible, New International Version*®. NIV®. Copyright © 1973, 1978, 1984 by International Bible Society. Used by permission of Zondervan Publishing House. All rights reserved.

Italics in Scripture quotations reflect the author's added emphasis.

Details in some anecdotes and stories have been changed to protect the identities of the persons involved.

ISBN 978-1-57856-821-5

Published in the United States by WaterBrook Multnomah, an imprint of the Crown Publishing Group, a division of Random House Inc., New York.

WATERBROOK and its deer colophon are registered trademarks of Random House Inc.

Library of Congress Cataloging-in-Publication Data
Burton, Valorie, 1973–
What's really holding you back? : closing the gap between where you are and where you want to
    be / by Valorie Burton.—1st ed.
      p. cm.
    ISBN 1-57856-821-8
    1. Self-actualization (Psychology)—Religious aspects—Christianity. 2. Success—Religious
aspects—Christianity. I. Title.
BV4598.2.B87 2005
248.4—dc22   2004024842

Printed in the United States of America
2012

10 9

*This book is dedicated
to two of my very best friends—
my parents, Leone and Johnny.*

*By your examples you have taught me
love, optimism, perseverance, character,
and unwavering faith in God.
I greatly admire you.*

Contents

Contents

Acknowledgments

I feel very blessed to have had the opportunity to write this book, to have it released by a publisher who truly cares about making a difference in people's lives, and to know that you are reading it. I wrote it for you, and so my first of many thanks goes to you. Yes, you! I am thankful for you and for all those I serve through writing, coaching, and speaking. Your encouragement and feedback and the struggles you've shared led me to know that this book needed to be written. Thank you for your love and appreciation. I value the opportunity to make a difference in your life.

Additional thanks go out to the following people:

- Laura Barker, my editor on behalf of WaterBrook Press. Your calm, peaceful spirit is a blessing! Thank you for helping me grow as a writer.

- My dad, Johnny A. Burton Jr. Thank you for passing on to me your youthful energy, positive attitude, and love for communicating with people. I appreciate you for blessing me with the foundation to live my life to the fullest and the confidence and encouragement to never hold back from my dreams.

- My mom, Leone Adger Murray. You are the most determined person I know. Watching you work hard to recover from the aneurysm and brain surgery in the prime of your life has strengthened my faith, inspired me to focus on what really matters, and taught me never to sweat the small stuff.

- Thanks to my brother Wade, for your work on my book tours. I love you and I'm excited about all the future holds for you!
- Most important, I thank God. I give You *all* of the glory for any transformation readers experience through this book, and I pray that they will do the same. The more You use me to inspire others, the more I grow into the person You created me to be.

It's Time for a Breakthrough

At age eleven I learned one of my first lessons on mustering courage in the face of fear. My parents, grandmother, and I were traveling near Estes Park, Colorado, on the highest paved road in the world. Grandmama had flown back to Denver with me after my summer with relatives in South Carolina, and Dad wanted to show her the sights. On our first stop that afternoon, we all got out of the car at a looking point. I ran to the edge of the road and peeked into the valley below. We were fourteen thousand feet above sea level, and the view before me gave literal meaning to the word "breathtaking." To my eyes' delight, I was looking down on the clouds.

But the second stop of our afternoon drive snatched my breath for an entirely different reason—and gave me a lesson that forms the foundation for this book, a lesson that will change your life if you embrace it.

As the winding roads grew steeper, the guardrails allegedly intended to prevent a car from plummeting south seemed inadequate to the task. Sitting in the back seat with me, Grandmama stretched her neck to peek out my window at the treacherous cliffs just a few feet from the road's edge. "Junior!" she said to my father while reaching into her purse for her blood pressure pills. "I appreciate the sightseeing tour, but I've seen enough now.

Let's turn around and go back down the mountain!" But the narrow road held no opportunities to reverse our course. And to make matters worse, I had to go to the bathroom. On a Sunday afternoon at fourteen thousand feet above sea level, few facilities were available. Finally after about fifteen minutes, we came upon a lodge. It was closed, but I was relieved to see five outhouses perched at the edge of the parking lot.

Dad parked the car, and I ran quickly to the row of portable bathrooms, which faced away from the parking lot. When I turned the corner at the end of the row, I was shocked to see a mammoth animal standing before me—much bigger than a horse and with large, flat antlers. We stared eye to eye for a moment—just long enough for me to resume breathing and realize I didn't really need to go to the bathroom that badly.

I backed up three steps, then took off running for the car. I jumped in and slammed the door behind me. "That was quick," my mom said. "What happened?"

"Oh, I don't have to go any more. I'm fine." Then I said matter-of-factly, "There's a moose behind the outhouses."

That was explanation enough for my parents. Dad cranked up the car. "I'm sure we'll find something when we get back to the bottom of the mountain."

My grandmother, however, wasn't having it. This woman, who grew up sharecropping and farming, wasn't afraid of much (except, apparently, steep Rocky Mountain roads). "Come on, here!" She grabbed my hand and opened the car door. When your southern grandmother demands that you "Come on, here!" it's generally a good idea to comply. So I slid out of her side of the car as my parents looked on, apparently as confident in her ability to tackle the situation as she was. As we walked across the parking lot, I got the feeling Grandmama was actually agitated with the moose, the way a parent might approach a teacher she felt had done her child wrong. Her confident body language said, "How dare this moose try to intimidate my grandbaby! If she wants to go to the bathroom, he's just going to have to get out of the way."

We turned the corner. The moose still stood there. This time it was him and Grandmama, eye to eye. She didn't look the least bit afraid, even though I'm pretty sure she'd never encountered a moose in Iva, South Carolina! Grandmama motioned her hand toward the moose as though she was swatting away a fly, and in her southern drawl, she spoke as if to a mangy mutt blocking the path to her own front porch: "Go on, now! Git!"

The moose turned and walked away about ten feet—just enough space for me to step into the stall with some degree of comfort. Then I came out and stood guard while Grandmama went in. I'd gotten my courage now! I wasn't afraid of the moose anymore. When she came out and we turned to walk away, the moose returned to his original spot.

The life lesson I learned that day is this: Fear needs only one antidote. That antidote is courage.

You may have your goal firmly in mind and your plans set, but as you turn the corner and start toward your destination, fear pops up like a giant moose, intimidating you and tempting you to run in the other direction. But when you talk back to your fear—whether yours is fear of failure or success, rejection or not being good enough—its power over you will be diminished. Life and death are in the power of the tongue. This is one of four themes threaded throughout this book: using your words wisely is a key to getting unstuck. You also need the wisdom to get help when you're stuck. You need bold people—people like my grandmother—who can give you courage. And you also need the perseverance to keep trying, to practice courage and, when you fail for whatever reason, to practice some more.

As my experience that Sunday afternoon so long ago illustrates, along life's journey you and I will experience breathtaking moments, winding roads, and enormous obstacles. Our job is to expect both the exciting moments and the fearful ones and to embrace the opportunity each offers to grow us into our full, God-give potential. This book shows you how. I will walk with you and coach you on your journey as you get unstuck and become unstoppable in every area of your life.

God has placed within each of us a driving passion along with the skills to accomplish our particular purpose and vision. But more than once along the way we will need to decide whether or not to embrace an adventure— one that will take us beyond our comfort zone but could also take us further along the path to success. These experiences offer us the opportunity to develop our character and broaden our perspective, taking us to a new place in life. But many times we succumb to our fears, giving up too quickly and easily rather than seizing the goals and desires of our heart.

Is Something Holding You Back?

In my life and executive coaching practice and throughout one of my earlier books, *Listen to Your Life,* I strive to help individuals explore their unique path in life—the path that makes the most of their natural gifts and talents, fulfills their life purpose, and leads to extraordinary success in every area of their life. But as I've talked with readers, coaching clients, and friends, I've learned that even those who know their purpose and recognize their path often appear to be paralyzed, unable to make progress toward their goals. Basically, there is a gap between where they are and where they want to be, and an invisible force seems to be holding them back.

Can you relate to this experience? Is there a gap between where you are in life and where you want to be? Do you feel as if an invisible force is holding you back from reaching your goals and achieving your dreams? The purpose of this book is to help you identify that force, to determine what's holding you back and then conquer it. It's time for a breakthrough!

I have found that when we muster up the courage to close an important gap despite our fears or doubts, we gain more than the reward of a goal reached. We gain depth of character and strength of courage. Through the process, we become more of the person God created us to be. Life is about so much more than what we achieve; it's about who we are and who we are becoming.

So how do you know when something is holding you back? Here are a few signs:

- Despite your passion or desire for something, you do not take steps to attain it.
- Others see more potential in you than you can see for yourself.
- You believe that others have held you back or hindered you in some way.
- You believe in your potential but are afraid to move toward it.
- You feel stuck.
- You are worried about embarrassing yourself.
- You are hiding behind shame or guilt.
- You have given up on certain goals or dreams because of something in your past.
- You allow fear to control your decisions.
- You sidestep issues that need to be addressed in order to avoid conflict or disappointment.

- You have talents you rarely use.
- You do not know your life purpose.
- You think or speak in negative terms about yourself, your abilities, and your goals.
- You are waiting on perfect circumstances before you take a step forward.

ARE YOU READY TO BREAK FREE?

At times we have trouble acknowledging, let alone conquering, the things that are holding us back. Some time ago as I was having dinner with a couple of new friends during a conference in Miami, the conversation turned to our individual goals and aspirations. As I laid out my hopes for the future, both friends listened attentively. They were enthusiastic and encouraging as they acknowledged that they could see the vision I had described to them. Although the hopes I shared seemed major to me, clearly they had no problem imagining me accomplishing them. One friend, a business coach named Andrew Morrison, founder of SmallBusinessCamp.com, even seemed perplexed that I had not already accomplished some of the goals I mentioned. Looking directly at me, he said in a matter-of-fact tone, "What's *really* holding you back, Val?"

I was taken aback by the question and immediately found myself feeling defensive. In our short conversation, he had not only discerned that I had the talent and ability to turn the vision into reality, he had also sensed that something was holding me back from doing so. "You have everything you need right now to accomplish that vision," he continued. "It's not more money or experience that you need. You need to get out of your own way."

He was absolutely right. I knew something was holding me back, but I didn't realize it was obvious to anyone else. When I returned to my hotel room that evening, I pondered his question. *What's really holding me back? Why did his question pierce my soul and leave me feeling so defensive?*

The explanation was very simple: fear of pain. All of us make decisions based on what we believe will either bring us joy or help us avoid pain. Specifically, I was avoiding the pain of rejection. My vision was too big to be accomplished on my own, which meant I would have to ask others for help. Actually, I perceived it as asking them for help, but in reality my ideas would be mutually beneficial. Nonetheless, there was a risk of being told no. So in order to avoid potential rejection, I had given up the pleasure of fully realizing the vision. Just as significantly, I clung to the illusion that I could do it alone—again out of fear of rejection. *If I do everything myself, then I won't need anyone else's help, I won't have to ask for anything, and therefore I'll avoid any possibility of rejection.*

The discussion that day prompted me to admit that not only were my patterns of behavior unhealthy, they were not God's will for my life. I was living in bondage, held back from reaching my own potential and, more important, from fulfilling God's purpose for my life at the highest possible level. How could I serve more people if I wasn't willing to risk being rejected by a few? To truly live out my vision and purpose, I had to move forward despite the fear that frantically screamed, "No! Don't go forward! People won't accept you yet! You need more money, more education, a bigger name!"

Have you, like me, found yourself held back by your desire to avoid pain? Perhaps the pain you fear isn't rejection but failure, worry, embarrassment, disappointment, loneliness, or another fear-based issue.

I believe this book is in your hands for a purpose. It's time for you to conquer the issues and challenges that are preventing you from living your best possible life. It's time to discover and break free from what's really holding you back. I intentionally ask, "What's *really* holding you back?" because most people give surface answers when asked what's keeping them from achieving their full potential. Here are some of the answers I hear most often:

- "I don't have enough time."
- "I don't have enough money."
- "I have kids. Their needs are holding me back."
- "I don't have the right experience or education."
- "I don't have the right background."
- "I don't have the right connections."
- "I'm not a good communicator."
- "I'm just bad at relationships...money...taking care of myself...or whatever!"

Some of these comments may echo your own response, but they do not reveal the deeper reasons behind your stagnancy. To effectively close the gap between where you are and where you want to be, you'll have to summon the courage to uncover the culprits that are holding you back and then take the necessary steps to break free. Of course, it's not enough to simply stop doing what isn't working in your life. You must also make changes so that you can start doing what *does* work. That's what I have set out to help you accomplish in this book.

How to Best Use This Book

This book is designed to help you uncover the challenges and invisible obstacles that hold you back and to help you overcome them. The answers are within your reach. My job as your coach is simply to provoke thought and help you explore the truth about yourself.

This book isn't intended to be read passively. If you want to close the gap between where you are and where you want to be, the words on these pages must be translated into action in your daily life. Each chapter poses a challenge that will bring you closer to overcoming the obstacles, fears, and misconceptions that threaten to hold you back from all that is possible for you. I'll be helping you identify specific action steps and learn from the results of those actions. This cycle of action and learning will empower you to accelerate the rate of your personal and spiritual growth.

Throughout the book, I will challenge you to take notice of four elements in your daily life that can either hold you back or—when used as God intends—propel you forward. These four elements are your thoughts, words, actions, and energy. You will boost your growth by eliminating the thoughts, words, actions, and energy-draining encounters that make you weak. You will replace those self-defeating habits with practices that place you in a position of strength. At the end of each chapter is a section titled Closing the Gap. This section contains four subsections—Focus Your Thoughts, Use Your Words Wisely, Target Your Actions, and Energize Your Spirit—that will help you immediately apply the principles you've learned in each area.

Focus Your Thoughts

Your thoughts are the birthplace of your words, actions, and energy. Throughout the Bible we are told of the importance of our thoughts. Philippians 4:8 states, "Whatever things are true, whatever things are noble, whatever things are just, whatever things are pure, whatever things are lovely, whatever things are of good report, if there is any virtue and if there is anything praiseworthy—meditate on these things." Everything you experience in life begins with a thought, whether the thought is yours or someone else's. The mind, and how you choose to use it, can answer the question of what's really holding you back and help you break free from it.

In this section, we will explore, in depth, the types of thoughts that need to be incorporated into your daily life as well as the types of thoughts you need to let go of. This section also offers a meditation point or idea to help focus your thoughts in the right direction. By renewing your mind with the truth of God's promises, you will be able to conquer whatever is keeping you from attaining your best possible life.

Use Your Words Wisely

Negative thoughts are reinforced when they are expressed verbally. But your own words aren't the only potential problem. The words of others often initiate thought patterns that can sabotage your success.

In this section we'll explore how to use your words for positive change and how to appropriately filter the words of others. I've also included exercises that will help you reflect on the words you use and equip you to choose your words carefully. As you work through these exercises, you'll learn how your words can serve as a tool to chip away the obstacles and issues that have held you back.

Target Your Actions

Your actions, or lack thereof, influence the circumstances of your life. If you want to change your life, you must be willing to change what you do on a daily basis. God has given you the power to make significant, positive changes because He has given you the power of choice! By taking consistent actions based on what you learn about yourself, you will transform your life.

One step at a time, you will move forward and break free from the invisible culprits that are holding you back. As you gain momentum, you'll find it easier to keep going! That's why I've included this section in each chapter, with specific steps to get you started. The key is to get yourself moving, and these exercises will do just that.

Energize Your Spirit

Just as a distance runner won't win a race by starting off like a sprinter, you also must manage your spiritual, physical, and emotional energy deliberately and for the long haul. As you break free of the restraints that have held you back, you will notice that the journey to complete freedom is a process. Identifying energy drainers is crucial to developing the strength to persevere, the attitude to overcome, and the power to live fully every day.

As we'll see, your most powerful source of energy is your spiritual connection. Sometimes we work hard to make changes and forget that our reliance on God is absolutely vital to our progress. Or perhaps we aren't sure how to pray about a particular issue. This section will help you articulate your needs to God and connect with Him in a powerful way.

As you go through each of the steps in this book, you may find it helpful to connect regularly with a partner or a few trusted friends. Some of the issues raised are going to challenge you at the deepest level. An encouraging partner who is working through the same process can help you stay focused.

You may want to pace yourself so that you don't become overwhelmed trying to make multiple changes at once. Consider reading one chapter a day or a few chapters each week, and use this book as a tool to truly transform your life by making lasting changes over time.

In addition, consider this book a resource that you can return to. As you will learn, breaking free from the issues that hold you back takes perseverance and conditioning. Just as you wouldn't win an Olympic competition by practicing once, you won't transform your life by doing something different just one time. You must recondition yourself to respond differently than you have in the past, and that will take patience, persistence, and practice! In some areas you may close the gap quickly as you sprint to the other side. In other areas you may crawl and meander, but you will still be moving forward! Any pace is better than remaining stuck and watching your dreams slip away.

I consider it a privilege to join you on your journey of moving from where you are to where you want to be. Let's get started!

One

Do You Know Where You're Going?

Identify Where You Want to Be

From the age of ten through high school, I lived in Denver, Colorado, a city with one of the most beautiful skylines in the world. The picture-perfect backdrop for Denver's skyscrapers is the snow-capped Rocky Mountains, which stand boldly on the horizon just fifty miles west of downtown. In addition to the great scenery they provide, the Rockies are a functional landmark. When I was a novice driver, the Rocky Mountains gave me a sense of direction. I found it impossible to ever get completely lost because I always knew which way was west! As a teenager I often wondered how people in other parts of the country without such an obvious landmark could figure out which direction they were going. The Rockies are also a popular destination. Hikers, skiers, and nature lovers flock to the Rocky Mountains every year as their vacation destination of choice.

Similarly, a specific destination and a clear sense of direction are critical to the pursuit of your life purpose. Identifying the overall vision for your life paves the way for determining the distance between where you are now and where you want to be, as well as the direction you need to take as you journey toward your goal. By keeping your eyes fixed on a specific goal or landmark, you can more easily maintain your focus and not lose your sense of direction.

What is your destination in life? Do you have a clear vision for where you are headed? Without one, it can be easy to ignore the gaps in your life. After all, if you aren't going anywhere in particular, why would it ever occur to you that you aren't where you want to be?

As you begin your journey to identify the things that are holding you back, I want you first to look to the horizon and explore possible destinations for your life. Take a few minutes to write out a paragraph describing your overall vision for the next stage of your life. What were you created to accomplish? What are your areas of passion? How would your life look if all of your skills and talents were being put to use on a regular basis? What would bring you the greatest sense of fulfillment? At this point, focus not so much on what you want to change as where you ultimately want to be.

Next, I want you to carefully observe where you are right now and compare it to where you want to be. Between here and there lies a gap that challenges you, perhaps even frightens you. To help you bridge that gap, let's look at five key areas of your life and explore how each of these can help you shape and reach your overall vision. What is your most important goal—your intended destination—in each of the following areas?

Your relationships:

Your career:

Your finances and resources:

Your physical health and environments:

Your spiritual life:

Taking the time to notice where you are and to determine where you want to be provides clarity. Lack of clarity can pose a serious stumbling block. As a life coach I often meet with clients who insist they are stuck, but when I ask them a few clarifying questions, I discover that they are stuck because they haven't taken the time to gain clarity about where they are, where they want to be, and what steps it would take to move from here to there. It sounds simple, but in the hectic pace of life, we can easily rush through our days in an unfocused, hazy state, overlooking key truths about our situation.

The State of Your Life assessment in the following chapter will help you explore this issue further and identify some of the gaps in your life.

Closing the Gap

Focus Your Thoughts
Visualize where you want to be in each of the five key areas of life listed earlier in this chapter. Keep your thoughts focused on the vision rather than on the obstacles that stand in your way.

Use Your Words Wisely
Write down your key goals in each of the five key areas of life, and post them where you will see them often—perhaps on your bathroom mirror, refrigerator, or desk, or in your appointment book.

Target Your Actions
Identify the landmark that will signal you have arrived where you want to be in your life. Consider some steps you can take to move in that direction.

Energize Your Spirit
God, please give me clarity regarding Your purposes and vision for my life. Help me step boldly into my destiny, trusting in Your wisdom to guide me along the way. Amen.

Two

Where Are You Now?

Determine the "State of Your Life"

The State of Your Life assessment is a simple measurement tool to gauge your progress in different areas of your life. I have included the five key areas of life—your relationships, career, finances and resources, physical health and environments, and spiritual life—that impact the "whole you." When any of these areas is lacking in your life or is draining your energy, it weakens your ability to move your whole life forward. By strengthening the basics of your life, you give yourself the energy and muscle to move forward and close gaps in all areas.

Following are twenty statements for each of the five key areas of your life. Check each statement that is true for you right now (not that you *wish* were true). Respond as honestly as possible. This isn't about getting a high "score"; it's about breaking free from what's holding you back. The only way to effectively do that is by embracing the truth. Please do not be concerned with what you may consider a low score. This is an opportunity to gauge where you are, pinpoint the gaps that exist between where you are and where you want to be, and measure your progress in the weeks ahead. You may be able to check only twenty-five of the one hundred statements today, but through adjustments in your thoughts, words, actions, and energy, you may find that in just a few weeks you will be able to check eighty-five statements.

In addition to this assessment, you may want to create a personalized assessment that reflects specific goals you have set. Simply write out in a journal the statements you would like to be able to check when you have closed the gap.

Relationships

____ If I needed a trusted confidant in a crisis, I have two or more people I can confidently call upon.

____ I do not feel manipulated in any way by people or circumstances.

____ No relationships are currently draining my energy.

____ I can say no with ease.

____ I feel connected in a meaningful way to my community.

____ I know that I am making a positive difference in other's lives on a daily basis.

____ I am on speaking terms with everyone in my family.

____ I feel loved.

____ I am not involved in any relationships that I feel I need to hide from anyone.

____ I feel free to say "I love you" in my closest relationships without any fear of rejection.

____ I am not withholding forgiveness from anyone.

____ I do not maintain friendships with people who only take from me but rarely give.

____ My relationships with my parents and/or children are peaceful and loving.

____ I am doing everything I can to be considered worthy of others' respect. My boss, co-workers, and/or customers treat me respectfully.

____ I am as nice to the janitor, receptionist, or cashier in a business as I am to the manager or president.

____ I do not gossip.

____ I tell others what I feel even when it is difficult or uncomfortable for me to do so.

____ When I have wronged someone, I always apologize and make amends.

____ There is no one in my life whom I am trying to change.

____ When someone offers constructive criticism, I listen without being defensive or arguing.

____ *Total number of statements about your relationships that you could truthfully make today*

Career

____ I love my work.

____ I feel "on purpose" when I am working.

____ There is no other work I would rather be doing than the work I am doing now.

____ I have a clear path to advancement.

____ I feel well compensated for my work.

___ I am at the top of my game.

___ I do not overwork.

___ I enjoy the people with whom I work.

___ I am not interested in changing careers in the next two years (that's careers, *not jobs*).

___ I have the education to qualify me for the type of position I aspire to.

___ Most people would consider me a role model of excellence in my work.

___ I am proud of my professional reputation.

___ I have no overdue projects looming at work.

___ I have a mentor or someone else who can answer my career questions and provide guidance.

___ My supervisors and/or clients are very pleased with my performance.

___ I rarely bring work home (once a month or less).

___ My work schedule suits my lifestyle.

___ I use my vacation time every year.

___ I have a compelling vision for my professional life.

___ My work does not consume my personal conversations.

___ *Total number of statements about your career that you could truthfully make today*

Finances and Resources

___ My finances do not cause me stress.

___ I pay off my credit-card balance in full each month (or I don't carry any credit-card debt at all).

____ I know exactly how much consumer debt I have, if any, and when it will be paid off. (For the purpose of this exercise, we will define consumer debt as credit cards, student loans, car loans, personal or home-equity loans, and personal debt other than your mortgage.)

____ I do not owe anyone money (or I am not avoiding any person or company to whom I owe money).

____ I have a plan to eliminate any debt I have accumulated, and I am following my plan. (Or I am currently debt-free and have a plan to stay out of debt.)

____ My credit report is a positive reflection of excellent financial habits.

____ I have not bounced a check in more than three years (or I have never bounced a check).

____ On a monthly basis, the amount of money I spend is at least 20 percent less than my income.

____ If I lost my job today, I could live off my savings for at least six months.

____ I have prepared a will to ensure that my assets are distributed according to my wishes after my death.

____ In the event of a major accident or illness, I have health insurance to cover my medical expenses.

____ In the event I become disabled, I have insurance that will replace at least 50 percent of my income.

____ I know my net worth.

____ I know when I plan to retire and how much money I will have at that point, and I am actively engaged in working toward that goal.

___ My life insurance and/or financial holdings are more than enough to ensure that my loved ones will not suffer financial loss in the event of my death.

___ Based on my connections, I feel confident in my ability to land a new job if necessary.

___ In my current line of work, I can chart a course that would allow me to double my income if I wanted to.

___ I tithe consistently.

___ I use my gifts and talents on a regular basis to give back to my community in a meaningful way.

___ I believe God is pleased with the way I handle the money and resources with which I've been blessed.

___ *Total number of statements about your finances and resources that you could truthfully make today*

Physical Health and Environments

___ I have had a complete physical within the past three years.

___ I am not afraid to go to the doctor.

___ My relationships are not causing me stress.

___ My blood pressure and cholesterol levels are within healthy limits, according to my doctor.

___ I exercise at least three times a week for thirty minutes or longer.

___ I laugh at least a few times every day.

___ I smile often each day.

___ When things are particularly difficult or challenging, I trust God rather than being worried and anxious.

___ I don't make a big deal out of small problems.

___ My home provides a clutter-free, supportive, safe, enjoyable environment for me.

___ My work environment is safe, clean, organized, and reflective of my values.

___ When driving, I am never aggressive or rude, nor do I act out in "road rage."

___ My car is consistently well maintained, clutter-free, and not a source of stress.

___ If I were in a health or family crisis, I have more than enough supportive family or friends to help me through it.

___ Based on medical recommendations, my weight is within the ideal range for my height.*

___ I eat healthy meals in regular intervals throughout the day.

___ Cardiovascular exercise is a part of my workouts.

___ I drink at least forty-eight ounces of water every day.

___ I do not use tobacco products or drugs, nor do I misuse alcohol.

___ I regularly set aside time for relaxing, having fun, and rejuvenating.

___ *Total number of statements about your physical health and environments that you could truthfully make today*

---

* According to the National Institutes of Health, the following formula works for both men and women in determining your body-mass index (BMI) and assessing total body fat, which is related to risk for disease and death: Multiply your weight in pounds by 705, then divide that number by your height in inches squared. So a person who is five-foot-eight and weighs 140 pounds would calculate it like this: (140 x 705) divided by (68 x 68) = 21.35. You are underweight if your BMI is less than 18.5; your weight is normal if your BMI is 18.5–24.9; you are overweight if your BMI is 25–29.9; and you are obese if your BMI is 30 or greater.

Spiritual Life

___ I am actively seeking to show God's love through the way I treat those around me and the way I carry out my responsibilities.

___ I seek ways to be of service daily.

___ I have a fulfilling relationship with God.

___ I am not easily annoyed or angered.

___ I pray daily.

___ My faith is stronger today than it has ever been.

___ I have stepped out on faith toward my vision despite my fears or doubts.

___ I am trusting God more completely to direct my steps and close the gaps in my life.

___ I am following God in every area of my life in which I have sensed Him leading me in a particular direction.

___ I am content with my life, but I also seek to live a better life.

___ I am not easily offended.

___ I am disciplined in maintaining my spiritual habits.

___ I know my life purpose.

___ I live my purpose on a daily basis.

___ I am constantly discovering opportunities for spiritual growth.

___ I am faithful over the "few things" God has placed in my care.

___ I study and meditate on God's Word regularly.

___ I am using the gifts God has given me to serve others in meaningful ways.

___ My life is filled with God's peace.

___ I enjoy my life.

____ *Total number of statements about your spiritual life that you could truthfully make today*

The State of Your Life
____ *Total score for all five areas of your life*

Now that you have identified the gaps between where you are and where you want to be—the specific targets you haven't reached—think for a moment about why you haven't closed these gaps before now. In the next chapter we'll talk about how you can turn your frustration about being stuck into power to forge ahead.

Closing the Gap

Focus Your Thoughts
Think back over the State of Your Life assessment. Of the statements you didn't check, which ones do you most wish you could have marked as being true?

Use Your Words Wisely
Repeat these words to yourself today: "Every day I am moving closer to my vision for my life."

Target Your Actions
Choose one statement from each area in the State of Your Life assessment that you want to address right away. Identify a step you can take to move toward making each statement true.

Energize Your Spirit
Lord, open my eyes to the gaps I need to close in my life, and give me the energy, strength, courage, and focus to close them. Amen.

Three

Are You Fed Up Yet?

Use Your Frustration to Fuel Your Turnaround

Karen was frustrated with her job. When she began working as a pharmaceutical sales representative right out of college, it had seemed a good use of her marketing degree. Although she enjoyed the commissions, she'd never been particularly excited about selling pharmaceuticals. After seven years in her job, she felt less qualified than ever to pursue the career path that had always intrigued her: advertising.

Then her boss, an excellent manager who had made the job bearable, left for another company. The new supervisor micromanaged his staff and seemed to enjoy making life difficult for everyone. He assigned Karen a new territory that required a forty-mile commute in bumper-to-bumper traffic. Given her supervisor's attitude toward her, Karen felt that the promotion she'd thought might be less than a year away was now unlikely. She was working more hours but not earning more money.

The frustration mounted. Karen began to dread getting out of bed in the morning. Finally, under the weight of her supervisor's increasing demands, Karen reached her breaking point. She recognized her frustration as a sign that it was time to make some changes. After sharing her dilemma with several friends and associates, she was eventually connected with someone who offered her a position at a top advertising agency—and a chance to move toward her longtime dream. She loved her new job and the opportunities it offered.

In the end, the only things that had held Karen back from her deeply desired career change during those years of feeling trapped in an unfulfilling job were her self-defeating thoughts and her reluctance to connect with the people who could open the right doors for her. When she finally got fed up with her situation, her frustration motivated her to seize the opportunities that may have been there all along.

As Karen learned, sometimes we simply have to get fed up with ourselves or our circumstances in order to break through to the next level. As you think about the areas in which you feel held back, ask yourself these two questions:

1. What aspect of my life bothers or frustrates me?
2. What am I willing to do about it?

Perhaps in the past you've been held back by complacency, willing to take a wait-and-see approach. But you've finally reached a breaking point when you say to yourself, "Something has to change. And whatever it takes, I will free myself from what's holding me back." If you're feeling frustrated, go with it! You don't have to remain stuck in an unsatisfying life. Instead, get fed up so you can move forward. Frustration is power.

Major change happens when you become so frustrated with your circumstances that you refuse to take it anymore. Think about it: A revolution does not occur when the people are satisfied. A revolution comes when irritations and frustrations have been bubbling for years. When a situation comes to a boil, people finally demand a change. They scream, "No more!" And they mean it.

The American civil rights movement of the 1950s and 1960s would not have happened if African Americans and others had been willing to continue putting up with injustice. Just a few generations removed from slavery, African Americans experienced more freedom, education, and opportunity than their forefathers ever dreamed. But they wanted—and deserved—more. Being relegated to second-class citizenship was not a burden they would willingly continue to bear. So they fought for change, for equality. The vision didn't become reality overnight, but African Americans were committed to achieving nothing less than justice for themselves, their children, and the generations to come. Their determination—and ultimately their success—was born of frustration.

When you figure out what is creating frustration in your life, you have taken the first step toward a breakthrough. Frustration can indicate that it's time for a change in attitude, direction, or focus. Rather than settling for disappointment or trying to force a situation to work, step back and ask yourself, "What options have I not considered?" In a relationship it could mean changing your attitude, becoming a better listener, or standing up for yourself. In your finances you may realize that in order to accomplish your goals, you'll have to increase your income or find the discipline to stop spending so much.

Let me share an example from my own life. My interest in writing books was initially sparked during my first semester of graduate school. As I pulled into the parking space in front of my apartment on that fall day in 1993, the thought of writing dropped into my mind out of the clear blue sky. Of course, ideas pass through my mind all the time, but this one really intrigued me. I immediately thought, "Yes! I would *love* to do that." I didn't know how or when, but in my spirit I just knew that thought had to become reality. I wouldn't rest until I had written a book.

Then, just two years later, I finally tackled my first draft. But after writing about ten thousand words, I was suddenly out of ideas! I had nothing more to say. Frustrated, I tabled the idea for a while.

Three years passed before I took any more steps forward. I created a book proposal for a different concept, attracted the interest of a literary agent, and began again. A publisher made a formal offer, but the deal never fully came together. I was disappointed, but quite frankly, it was just as well, because I couldn't seem to concentrate long enough to crank out the prose anyway. Something was holding me back, but I couldn't quite identify the culprit. Why was I always thinking or talking about what I was going to do but never actually *doing* it?

What was holding me back?

A few obvious answers came to mind: Hesitation. Laziness. Lack of time. Procrastination. Identifying these factors didn't seem to help, because even if I acknowledged that I was procrastinating or that I needed to rearrange my schedule to fulfill my dream, I still didn't make the effort to do it.

What was *really* holding me back was *me.* I was in my own way. Eventually I became disgusted with my procrastination and weary of talking about my dream without getting any closer to it. Only when I finally got sick and tired of my excuses and clarified my purpose for writing was I released from the grip of my own self-sabotage.

At long last I just sat down and got to work. I eliminated the excuses and found the time to write. Yes, I had a business to run, but the truth is, I had been using that to justify my procrastination. There would always be some demand on my time, some other worthy project I could be tackling. The question was, what did I most want to accomplish? I had to align my actions with my priority of writing a book. I set aside time at night and on the weekends, and in just two months, I finished my manuscript. Amazingly, the process that had seemed so complicated in my mind was in reality a joy!

Deciding to move toward your goal is essential to getting unstuck. Allow your frustration to kick-start you and propel you a few steps forward. By just getting yourself in motion, you'll gain encouragement. You'll draw strength from your actions as you begin to manifest change in your life. And your frustration will dissipate as you recognize your own potential to move past the frustration toward a productive solution.

Closing the Gap

Focus Your Thoughts

Even as you pursue God's purposes for your life, you may experience frustration and failure. But He will sustain you through it. As you learn from your disappointments, He will use them to shape your character and refine your vision. As you allow today's frustrations to fuel tomorrow's fulfillment, meditate on this scripture: "The steps of a good man are ordered by the LORD, and He delights in his way. Though he fall, he shall not be utterly cast down; for the LORD upholds him with His hand" (Psalm 37:23-24).

Use Your Words Wisely

Take notice of how often your words feed your frustration. Listen for comments such as "I hate this job" or "I'm so sick of this!" When you find yourself tempted to speak this way, instead rephrase your words as forward-focused questions such as, "What am I willing to *do* about this situation?"

Target Your Actions

Today, take one specific action toward improving the situation that frustrates you most. It may mean making time for fifteen minutes of exercise, refusing to engage in an argument when someone pushes your buttons, or moving forward when you want to procrastinate. Whatever your frustration, identify at least one positive action for overcoming it—and then take it!

Energize Your Spirit

Dear God, please help me turn my frustration into positive power. I am tired of being stuck, and I know it is not Your will for my life. From this day forward, endow me with the strength, desire, and wisdom to overcome the restraints. Give me the conviction to confront my challenges rather than shrink from them. I want to build momentum, and I thank You in advance for helping me do just that. Amen.

Four

Are Your Goals Vivid and Specific?

Develop a Clear Strategy

Vagueness in your goals or vision creates a thick fog that prevents you from seeing what your next steps or the best route might be. Vivid and specific goals, by contrast, empower you and bring clarity to your decisions. They create a sense of purpose and direction. Having a clear objective also empowers others to more easily recognize how they can help you.

Bill Gates, founder of Microsoft, set forth a clear-cut vision in the 1980s: a personal computer on every desk and in every home, all running Microsoft software on a Microsoft operating system. It was an extremely bold, over-the-top vision at a time when the idea of a personal computer was just beginning to take shape. But it was a vision that everyone within the company could rally around. No matter what one's individual role was, employees could see a greater purpose in their work. They could envision themselves as part of the grand plan. Today, more than twenty years later, Microsoft has made incredible progress toward realizing its founder's vision.

Whether you're uncertain about your next steps or simply feeling stuck, a specific and vivid vision can help launch you toward success. Clear, compelling goals that excite and challenge you will serve as a source of strength. Knowing that you want to succeed is not enough. You need a clear definition of success that includes the goals you're willing to fight for.

Consider the following seven principles as you develop your strategy for moving toward where you want to be.

1. Be clear about your vision. Paint a mental picture of what your ideal life will look like three months from now, one year from now, and five years from now. Your vision should compel you to take action and move forward. It should include every area of your life—relationships, career, finances and resources, physical health and environments, and spiritual life.

2. Set specific written goals. Goals that are written down are far more likely to be remembered. Writing them down gives you an opportunity to think things through, expand on your intentions, and reread them regularly. As you write out your goals, strive to include as much detail as you can. Vague goals lead to failure and frustration, while specific objectives are more likely to lead to success. Be precise about what you want and how you will define success. For example, "I want to make more money" is vague. "I want to increase my income by 30 percent in the next twelve months and double it within three years" is specific—and measurable. You'll know without a doubt whether you have achieved your objectives.

3. Set only those goals you feel led to pursue. Don't chase a goal because others feel you should or because it seems like "the thing to do." Instead, listen to what your life is telling you. Allow peace to guide you in your decisions. If you experience inner turmoil about a goal—true unrest, not just the usual fears—trust your spirit and hold off on the goal, or drop it altogether. Your goals should stretch you and get you excited about your life. Follow your heart and pursue goals that allow you to fully express the essence of who you are and that lead you to fulfill God's purposes for your life.

4. Drop any goals that lead you away from your vision. Once you have clarified your vision and your definition of success, test every goal by asking yourself, "Does this lead me closer to my vision?" Don't allow yourself to be distracted by old goals that no longer fit your new vision or by new opportunities that will lead you in the wrong direction. For example, if you have made it a goal to focus a more significant portion of your time on your family during this season of life, you may need to turn down an offer to serve in a leadership position that would distract you or drain your energy. It may be admirable and even fun to coach the Little League team or sit on the board of some community organization, but you only have so much time in your days. Prioritizing that time means being willing to say no to the activities that don't lead you toward your primary objectives.

5. Set a deadline, then create a time line. Just as it's important to set vivid and specific goals, it's crucial to be clear about your method for reaching those goals. How will you go about accomplishing them? What must you focus on first? Many people are held back because they make the achievement of the goal too complicated. Start by setting a deadline, then creating a time line with the specific steps you must take to achieve the deadline. Jump right into the goal by getting specific about what you must do to achieve it!

If you don't identify a time and a date by which you want to meet your goal, you'll be tempted to procrastinate, always referring to it as something you want to do "someday." To make certain your someday comes sooner rather than later, set a reasonable deadline. Be sure that it's not so soon that you become overwhelmed or discouraged or so far away that you'll indefinitely postpone taking action.

After setting your deadline, create a time line by breaking down your objective into individual steps with mini-deadlines that will lead you toward your goal. An organized time line discourages procrastination and enables you to comfortably meet your deadline.

6. Let go of all excuses as to why you can't reach the goal. A compelling vision requires faith. Resist the temptation to shoot down all of your "big ideas" with excuses as to why they cannot be achieved. Instead, embrace those ideas with an attitude that believes all things are possible. Excuses are based in fear, which can be your biggest enemy on the road to success. We'll address how to overcome fear in an upcoming chapter. For now, I simply ask you to throw out your excuses and cast a vision that requires you to dream big.

7. Maintain your focus. Many goals are abandoned prematurely when people give in to fears, doubts, misperceptions, and discouragement. To achieve the success you desire, you must maintain your focus. Post your goals in places you will see them often. Then stick with your plan and keep moving forward. Your vision may not become reality as soon as you'd like, but have patience and never give up. Those who stay in the race are the only ones who cross the finish line!

Closing the Gap

Focus Your Thoughts
Consider your top goals and determine where you need to be more specific about your objectives.

Use Your Words Wisely

In the next two days, identify three to five specific goals—including dead-lines—that will bring your vision to life. Write them down and post them in a place where you will be reminded of them daily.

Target Your Actions

What is your top goal for the next twelve months? This week, take the next step that will move you toward your target. Be strategic about your actions, and pursue only those that will lead you to success.

Energize Your Spirit

God, I ask You to give me wisdom and clarity about how to pursue Your purposes for my life. Keep me from being scattered and vague. Help me narrow my goals and maintain my focus in spite of distractions, discouragement, and adversity. Amen.

Five

What Are Your Nonnegotiables?

Refuse to Lower Your Standards

Certain aspects of your vision are so integral to who you are and what you believe that you simply can't afford to compromise or settle for anything less. You look straight toward the goal without doubting or questioning it. You don't wonder about your alternatives because no other options will suffice. These are your nonnegotiables.

At age thirty-four Sheryl was so tired of the way her life was going that she decided she wouldn't settle for it any longer. She set some goals for herself that were not subject to change. As a teenager growing up in the projects, Sheryl had been an honor student. But she and her longtime boyfriend let their sexual curiosity get the best of them. Sheryl became pregnant, got married, and dropped out of school at age fifteen. Ten years later she was divorced and pregnant with her ninth child. The family was living on a welfare check of just three hundred dollars a month. By the time she was thirty-four and a mother of nine, Sheryl was fed up with struggling, and a chance conversation with a grocery-store clerk inspired her to create a vision for a better future. Going back to school would be her ticket, and for Sheryl that goal was not up for negotiation.

I met Sheryl, now in her sixties, during a speaking engagement in 2002. As she described her vision for her life, she told me that she had decided that being an example for her children—showing them that with God anything is possible if you focus and persevere—was nonnegotiable. "I didn't want them to be worried about taking care of their mother later in life," she explained. "I wanted them to dream and to believe in themselves. And I wanted to lead by example."

Sheryl went back to tenth grade, attending school in the summer and the evenings, and riding the same yellow school bus as children less than half her age. She didn't have a car or extra money for transportation. Despite a house fire that destroyed everything she owned, Sheryl didn't give up. On track to graduate with honors, she applied and was accepted at a state university.

Then, just a short time before Sheryl's graduation from high school, her eighteen-year-old son was murdered in a seemingly random act of violence.

"It was the most horrible, horrible feeling to lose my child," she told me. "I wanted to quit school."

But she knew her son had wanted her to finish. So finding strength from God, she did. She earned a bachelor's degree in social work—again with honors. Then she went on to earn a master's in social work. She was determined to help women whose experiences mirrored her own—single mothers struggling to make ends meet. When I last spoke to her, she was working as a counselor and employment resource specialist in a welfare-to-work program. She serves her community, inspiring others by her example of sticking to and achieving her nonnegotiable goals.

I love sharing Sheryl's story because it proves that when you decide you *must* have something, you will refuse to allow anything to hold you back.

What are the nonnegotiables in your life? Consider the five key areas—your relationships, career, finances and resources, physical health and environments, and spiritual life—and ask yourself, "What is it that I absolutely must have?" Knowing the answer to this question will help you establish boundaries and rules that will empower you to press forward despite fears, obstacles, and challenges. Here are a few nonnegotiables you might consider incorporating into your overall life strategy:

- I must maintain a healthy weight.
- I must pursue God's purpose for my life.
- I must achieve my educational goals.
- I must get my financial life in order.
- I must tithe my income.
- I must be respected in my relationships.
- I must spend quality time with my children every day.

Whether you adopt one or more of these along with nonnegotiables on your own list, the goals you establish as nonnegotiable should be the ones that most reflect your values. Often they echo the standards you learned from your family. Expressing respect for and receiving respect from others is one of my nonnegotiables I can trace back to my childhood. From listening to my parents' conversations and observing their actions, I learned to be respectful of others while simultaneously expecting to be respected by those I encountered, regardless of their status or position. When I entered the work world, and later the entrepreneurial world, my nonnegotiable view of giving and receiving respect was essential in building successful business relationships. Had I wavered under pressure, it would have impacted my credibility and even my financial bottom line.

Our nonnegotiable values and goals also can be shaped by previous life lessons or painful experiences. In chapter 3, I explained how frustration can be a catalyst for change. Nonnegotiable goals are sometimes born when you become so frustrated by a situation that you vow to never again find yourself in that position. Like Sheryl, you can allow your frustration to birth a drive in you that says, "Never again will I go through the struggles I've endured. I'm going to do what it takes to set my life up for success."

Nonnegotiable stances are not about being inflexible and difficult to work with. They are about standing for something. They help define what you are about. They push you forward naturally because they are driven by your beliefs about what your life should be. Nonnegotiables are your minimum standards, the bar you set. Make certain such goals reflect your own standards and not those of others.

It takes strength to push through whatever is holding you back. You build your strength, in part, by stretching yourself, taking consistent action, and meeting a personal level of expectation that prepares you for the next level. Pray about what goals should be nonnegotiable in your life. Let God guide you, then follow Him.

Closing the Gap

Focus Your Thoughts
Think back on your actions and decisions during the past month. At any time have you dropped goals and values that are important to you in exchange for something that requires less commitment, fear, or sacrifice?

Use Your Words Wisely

Stop for a moment and think about the goals that are "musts" for you, the objectives you're not willing to downsize or abandon for something easier. Write out a list of your nonnegotiables and, beside each goal, note why you aren't willing to compromise in this area.

Target Your Actions

Pull out your appointment calendar and compare it with your list of non-negotiables. Make adjustments where needed to ensure you're allowing the time you need to accomplish your key goals.

Energize Your Spirit

Dear God, give me the strength to hold fast to my dreams and the commitment to stop wavering in the face of adversity. Help me establish goals that are in keeping with my values and with Your intentions for my life. Amen.

Six

What's Your Motivation?

Realize Your Purpose Is Not About You

E arly in my career I was focused on how great it would be to achieve certain goals—getting a book published, doing media interviews, speaking to particular audiences, earning a certain amount of money. My decisions were driven by the rewards I anticipated from being successful.

A pivotal point in my career came when I finally realized that my work was not about me. God had placed within me specific skills and passions not for the purpose of making me successful but to make a difference in others' lives through my success. Yet I had been focused on personal rewards and achievement rather than on God's purposes and praise. I hadn't even been aware of my attitude until one day, while praying about all the things I wanted to see happen, it hit me. Or rather, the Holy Spirit hit me with a bit of revelation: *Your purpose isn't about you.*

God doesn't even need you to achieve it. He can accomplish His purposes through whomever He chooses. It was a humbling thought, and I needed to hear it. I accepted this truth, recognizing what a blessing it is to serve others as God directs.

Ultimately, all of us have the same purpose: to touch the lives of others in a way that only we can. Your success is not measured by accolades and impressive achievements. True success involves learning, growing, and being a vessel through which others are blessed by your unique gifts, talents, and experiences. If you won't step up to the plate, God will use someone else. His plans can and will be accomplished, whether or not you and I choose to participate. But we should be inspired to live our purpose simply because it is what God created us for. This must be our motivation: to serve, to make a difference, to help others experience God's love when they have an encounter with us.

Of course, it's healthy to have goals, but we should never lose sight of the fact that we are here to serve. Through your special way of bringing people together or your unique talent for music or your gift for building businesses and creating jobs, you can serve by touching the lives of others. What impact have you made through your words and actions? Is it positive and meaningful? If not, what would make it more so?

In a world that is overwhelmingly focused on what you have, what you drive, and how much prestige you have, we can easily make the mistake of placing more value on what we get than on what we give. What drives your desire to close the gap between where you are and where you want to be? What *really* drives you? Be honest with yourself about your motives. Do any of the following play a role in your motives? (Circle all that apply.)

receiving praise from others

gaining prestige

accumulating money

achieving popularity, fame, or
    notoriety

proving a point

attention

receiving recognition

remaining in my comfort zone

being thought of as important

ego

meeting someone else's
    expectations

gaining status

having access to certain people

competing with someone else

other _____

other _____

other _____

You may wonder why motives matter if our intentions are good and we aren't deliberately harming anyone else as we strive to achieve our own goals. Motives are important because we derive our energy from them. Motives serve as the fuel that keeps us going in the pursuit of our vision. If that fuel is tainted, we cannot fulfill our potential or fully engage in our purpose—and we'll create a polluted, unhealthy environment for ourselves and those around us.

Have you ever admired someone from afar and then discovered that person wasn't who she appeared to be? You believed she was acting out of a love for blessing others, but when you saw her up close, her words, attitude, or actions made it obvious that she was simply looking out for herself. Perhaps she started out with a genuine desire to serve, but popularity, money, and status clouded her perspective. Eventually she began to believe that her talents were there to serve her own purposes and that other people were there to serve her needs rather than the other way around.

Many years ago my parents attended an event featuring a famous and highly acclaimed actress. When her performance ended and she had the opportunity to interact with the attendees, she was extremely curt with her fans, including my parents. My parents never forgot how she had treated them. In fact, they vowed never to support another of her movies or shows. They were deeply disappointed that she was not who she appeared to be on stage and in front of the camera. To this day when I see this actress, my view of her is tainted.

How much more responsible are you as a Christian to ensure that others do not see in you the impure motives so common in the world? You can do more harm than good by proclaiming your faith but not living up to it. Just as important, when the fuel that drives you is tainted, you will make it only so far in life. You may appear to be highly successful, but your spirit will find itself empty, exhausted, and sputtering.

In those areas in which your motives are tainted, how could you change your attitude to one of service? For example, if you have been saying no to God in some area of your life because of self-interest or fear, clearly your motives are impure. You may be responding out of fear, or you may be seeking to satisfy your own desires rather than serve God's will for your life.

Impure motives are never about God's will; they are always about our own desires or fears. On the other hand, when we allow ourselves to be directed by God's objectives, He empowers us to accomplish things we could never do on our own. That power grows more potent when our energies are invested in service.

The more willing you are to serve, the more opportunities will come knocking on your door. When you are driven by the desire to serve others, you have tapped into pure energy, the driving force behind the purpose for which you were created.

Watch what happens when you adopt an attitude that says, "In everything I do, I will seek to be of service." When you take the focus off yourself, you'll often find that you feel lighter. The burden of constantly seeking your own way and taking it upon yourself to fill the voids in your life is lifted. When you seek to be of service, others sense your pure motives. They observe your sincerity, and that often brings with it more opportunities to be of service. In fact, service opportunities seem to flock to such individuals, perhaps because it is so rare to find people driven to serve. So many needs in this world are going unmet. If every person fulfilled even a portion of what they were created to do, we would see incredible transformation in people's lives.

Let go of the motives that serve only your purposes. And when praise, money, status, and recognition come as a result of your success, make sure that such symbols do not become the driving force in your life. Instead, be motivated by the possibility that your life and your vision will serve a higher purpose—one that will be a blessing in the lives of others.

Closing the Gap

Focus Your Thoughts
Take notice of any impure motives that may be driving you. Ask God to fill your mind with His thoughts of compassion for others and ideas for how you can serve them in His love.

Use Your Words Wisely
Remind yourself daily, "In all that I do, I will seek to be a blessing, not a hindrance, in the lives of those I encounter."

Target Your Actions
Refuse to act on anything that is driven by impure motives.

Energize Your Spirit
Lord, Your Word says that if I will delight myself in You, You will give me the desires of my heart [Psalm 37:4]. Give me motives that are pure and the desire to be of service as I move toward my vision. Rather than turning to the unhealthy opportunities and false promises of this world, I trust You to satisfy my spirit. Amen.

Seven

Are You Treating the Symptom or the Problem?

Pinpoint the Source of Your Challenges

Imagine that you've been experiencing pressure near your eyes, along with a runny nose and a headache. You suspect you're suffering from a sinus infection, and you'd like some relief from your discomfort, so you schedule a visit to your doctor. After a brief examination she announces, "Well, looks to me like you have a runny nose and some sinus pressure."

Your response would probably be to look at her as if she were crazy. "Yeah, uh, I know that, Doctor. That's why I came to you for a diagnosis." You don't want the doctor to merely acknowledge your symptoms; you want her to pinpoint the cause and, more important, give you a remedy for eliminating the symptoms altogether.

This scenario is all too real for many of us who are attempting to self-medicate when we're feeling sluggish in our journey toward success. We often identify the symptom as the problem. "I don't have enough time," we may complain. Or "I don't have enough money," "I don't have the right connections," "My family doesn't approve," "I need more…"—you fill in the blank.

The fact is, unless we get to the root of the problem and deal with it honestly, we're going to continue floundering. Yet too many of us fixate on the symptoms, or perceived problems, in our lives rather than identifying the true source of our challenges. For example, if you were to tell me that money (or a lack thereof) is holding you back, I would ask you to rethink your conclusion. Although it may not be pleasant to hear, if you have had *ongoing* struggles with your money, the issue most likely is not the money but your approach to it. More important, the root problem may be what drives the choices you make. Likewise, if you come to me with *ongoing* relationship struggles and insist that your partner needs to change, I would challenge you to reflect on the choices you have made that are contributing to your problem. Those relationship problems are a symptom of a deeper issue that is holding you back.

It's intimidating, even humbling, to confront the hurdles in our path. But we need to recognize that if you and I are moving purposefully, fulfilling the divine mission we were sent here to complete, there will always be forces at work trying to hold us back from our destiny. The key is to identify the ways in which those forces prey on our insecurities, fears, and weaknesses.

Take a look at the following list and circle any of the issues that may be presenting a roadblock in your journey toward fulfillment:

fear of failure	lack of focus
fear of success	lack of personal growth
fear of rejection	lack of spiritual growth
fear of inadequacy	lack of faith
laziness	need for approval
pride	complacency
pessimism	guilt
negativity	shame
lack of purpose	avoidance

In all likelihood, just one or two specific issues are at the root of your struggles to move forward. The problem is that just one issue can manifest itself in a multitude of ways. A fear of inadequacy can manifest itself in overachievement, perfectionism, weak boundaries, insecurity, and/or a fear of rejection. Each of these manifestations can result in daily thoughts and actions that hold you back in a variety of ways. That's why, in the pages ahead, I'll be guiding you through the practice of self-curiosity—questioning your behavior and exploring ways to uncover the invisible culprit that holds you back.

Why bother with all this? you may wonder. Because your life isn't just about you and what you want. It is about growing fully into the person you were created to be so that you can fulfill your highest purpose and potential. You can't do that if you continually allow your insecurities to cause you to shrink from the opportunities before you. If you allow your fears to control you and your weaknesses to overpower you, you will never close the gap between where you are and where you want to be.

Closing the Gap

Focus Your Thoughts

Look back at the issues you identified as possible roadblocks on your road to fulfillment. Search the Bible for a verse that addresses one of those issues. (For example: If one of your root issues is fear that manifests itself as negativity, you might choose Philippians 4:8.) Then meditate on that verse until it seeps into your thought life.

Use Your Words Wisely

Take out your journal and ponder the question, "What's *really* holding me back?" Strive to look beyond the symptoms to the deeper issues behind your choices.

Target Your Actions

Take note of an area in your life in which you've been thinking, "I can't because…" Then make a list of all the reasons you can—and then do it!

Energize Your Spirit

God, grant me the perseverance to press forward until I uncover every misconception, obstacle, and fear that threatens to hold me back. Give me the strength to persist until I uncover it. When I do, help me understand the issue and purge it from my life. Amen.

Eight

Have You Asked Yourself the Right Questions?

Uncover the Answers at the Heart of Your Issues

In the previous chapter I mentioned a concept called self-curiosity. It is the process of questioning your feelings, emotions, and behavior so that you can better understand yourself. You must be willing not only to pinpoint the source of your problems but also to question why you are struggling with an issue—and be honest with yourself in your answers. Self-curiosity invites us to face our own truth, our own fears, and our own humanity.

This concept is so important to your personal and spiritual growth. While it can be easy to throw out some reasons why things are the way they are, our first responses are usually the surface answers: "They won't let me." "God hasn't opened the door for me yet." "It's too expensive." But when you probe further out of a desire to know the truth, you will discover the deeper answers. That truth will set you free to move forward in specific areas of your life.

In addition to addressing the challenging questions raised throughout this book, you can practice self-curiosity by writing through an issue. When I say "writing through it," I simply mean that you sit down with pen and paper, or at your computer, and begin to write what you feel. Then, after reviewing what you've just put on paper or on the computer screen, you begin asking, "What's that about?"

To get to the heart of the truth, you can employ three types of self-curiosity questions: Probing questions, expansive questions, and action questions. *Probing questions* dig beneath the surface to uncover the reasons for your behavior or thoughts:

- "What am I afraid of?"
- "Why am I afraid?"
- "What message could my emotions be sending me?"
- "What's my excuse for not taking action?"

Expansive questions challenge you to think bigger and envision your possibilities:

- "What would it feel like to reach the goal I have been held back from?"
- "If I could spend every day doing work I love, what would that look like?"
- "How could I have more impact in the lives of those around me?"
- "If nothing was holding me back, what would I do with my life?"
- "What's possible for my life that I have not pursued?"
- "What legacy do I want to leave?"

Action questions move you past the planning and exploration stage or help you get unstuck in a particular area:

- "What, specifically, could I do to move beyond the things that are holding me back?"
- "What could I do to reduce my risk of failure?"
- "How might I best use my gifts and abilities to fulfill my life purpose?"
- "What is the next step I need to take to move forward?"
- "What is my deadline for taking the next step?"
- "Who is my role model, and what steps did he or she take to reach the goal I want to reach?"
- "What actions have I been taking that are not working? What can I do differently, and when will I take action?"

I'm amazed by the truths I discover about myself every time I do this. By being brutally honest, I uncover the answers I need to get unstuck. Sometimes I may not be ready for the answer, but nonetheless it comes.

To illustrate the power of self-curiosity in uncovering the real issues in our lives, let me share a personal example from my journal, dating back to the early days of pursuing my mission as my full-time work. This was a crucial time in my life, but often the path ahead was murky. At one point I found myself exhausted, frustrated with my progress, and concerned about how to make ends meet financially. A nine-to-five position felt like the easy way out. I was on the verge of accepting a full-time position with a company and pursuing my vision only part time. I wanted to make more money and had decided that was the issue driving me to consider abandoning my path. But I wasn't quite ready to give up on what I believed was God's vision for my life. I decided to get curious and uncover the real issues. Here's an excerpt of what I wrote:

I've been questioning myself about what's wrong. Why do I feel like "jumping ship"? I know my feelings of giving up are premature because, quite frankly, there is some "low-hanging fruit" that I have not yet tried to pick. Why? Because it is easier to stay stuck in my comfort zone and make excuses about why I cannot have what I want and what God wants for me. It's easier to explain to people that God isn't opening the doors when indeed He has given me the ideas, the contacts, the intelligence, and the time to accomplish His mission for my life.

So what's missing? What's the problem *really?* The problem is that perhaps I don't want to change my ways. I need to create structure in my life—especially in my work life. I need more discipline. I've been so blessed to have the freedom to do things when I want and how I want that perhaps I've been spoiled, a victim of my own success and blessings. But the fruit of the Spirit includes self-discipline. Our God is a God of order. The fruit of the Spirit also includes long-suffering. That's patience. You don't usually get what you want overnight.

So what am I struggling with? Who am I struggling with? I am struggling with God—and it is the will of the Enemy. Ooh! That's powerful. The Enemy wants me to struggle against God, to feel frustrated and confused, to blame and make excuses. The Enemy has told me that all things are *not* possible. And I have chosen to believe him. Why have I believed this lie? Am I living in God's will or the Enemy's? Have I fallen into his trap of deception? Have I been blaming God for things not going exactly as I believed they would when in fact I haven't done all that I could, haven't fully listened to my life and taken action based on what I've heard? Ouch!

57

Perhaps the reason I am struggling is because I know what I am capable of—and it is more than I am producing right now. It is painful to be pregnant with possibility yet unable to give birth. Hmm…pregnant with possibility yet unable to give birth? Am I unable or uncooperative? I am so close to giving birth that the pains are getting intense. It's time to push, and I'm scared to push! I know that it is my responsibility to allow myself to be stretched beyond my previous limits. I can feel all of this potential inside, yet I have refused to stretch so that I can create the room it needs to come out. That can't be God's will. That can only be my personal limitations.

After exploring what was holding me back by writing through it—practicing self-curiosity—I decided that rather than jumping ship, I needed to dig my heels in deeper and keep going. The Lord never promised me the journey would be a piece of cake. He only promised that it would fulfill His purpose for my life, using my gifts, talents, and experiences. In fact, how on earth would I teach others if I didn't learn from my own issues and struggles?

As you can see, by asking question after question, I discovered that my concerns about money were just a surface excuse; the real issue was fear. In writing through my frustration, I learned some negative truths about myself that I needed to address. I decided that until I had fully dealt with those issues, I did not have the right to give up. Accepting a corporate job would not have been God's perfect will for my life. I needed to stay on the path, pursuing my mission full time, because it was all part of God's plan to mold me into the person He needed me to be.

Sure, I wanted to make more money, but I had enough. I had simply bought into the lie that ensnares so many of us—the mistaken belief that our lives and our decisions are about us, our preferences, our comfort. As we saw in chapter 6, God has designed us for a higher purpose than our own satisfaction; He wants to use us to influence and help others. And contrary to what the world may claim, we will find true freedom when we stop making excuses and simply do what God has asked us to do. Remember, He never calls us to accomplish something without equipping us for the task.

Journaling as a form of prayer, meditation, and self-curiosity can reveal key issues and unlock the answers you've been seeking. When you feel confused, frustrated, or stuck, write! Don't worry about writing well. Just get your frustration out of your head and onto paper or a computer screen. Ask yourself the difficult questions and be truthful in your answers. Then you'll feel the restraints that have held you back begin to lose their grip.

Closing the Gap

Focus Your Thoughts
Just for today, turn off the radio, the CD player, the television, or whatever background noise usually distracts you from self-examination. Turn your thoughts to what you'd like to see in key areas of your life and what stands in your way.

Use Your Words Wisely
Spend some time journaling. Concentrate on thinking through the challenges you face, asking questions to take you beyond surface answers to the heart of the truth.

Target Your Actions

Based on what you've learned through journaling and self-curiosity, identify one decision you can make to move forward in a key area of your life. Then determine to act on that choice today.

Energize Your Spirit

Lord, please bring to my mind the probing and expansive questions I need to answer. Give me the courage and wisdom to find the answers that will enable me to move forward in the direction You are leading me. Amen.

Nine

How Much Influence Do Your Emotions Have?

Let Your Feelings School You, Not Rule You

Melanie was beautiful, energetic, and hardworking. At age thirty-one, she had her own consulting business and was a super sales-person, pulling down $150,000 annually handling projects for a variety of companies. When I met her, she was madly in love and talked incessantly about her boyfriend—except when she was rehashing the details of her recently failed marriage to her third ex-husband. She seemed to have it together in so many ways, but I was perplexed by her complex love life. She described it in very romantic terms. "I love being in love," she commented, before asking, "When are you going to get married? You'd make a great mom."

Why is she so fixated on marriage? I wondered. It seemed that love, or at least her version of it, was like a drug. She was hooked on the feeling, and that feeling had already steered her toward the altar three times before her thirtieth birthday. She had a simple explanation for why each union didn't work. The first one "couldn't fully commit." The second "wasn't faithful and was a little abusive." The third "became a different person" after they got married, she said. Of course, the current boyfriend was perfect, according to her. I probed to see if he had any faults at all, but she couldn't seem to name any. Like the other relationships, this one was a whirlwind that would take her to the altar.

Our friendship had centered mostly on business, and after she married for the fourth time, we lost touch. About six years later, I ran into her while shopping. Not surprisingly, she reported that her fourth marriage had ended. He said he'd "fallen out of love" with her. But she had a new boyfriend, wonderful and perfect in every way.

Like Melanie, many people allow their feelings to control the most critical decisions of their lives. I hope your situation isn't that extreme, but I imagine that if you look back at some of the decisions you most regret, you'll probably find that your emotions played a bigger role than your intuition, knowledge, and wisdom. Perhaps you entered a bad relationship based on your feelings or ended a relationship that could have been salvaged. Perhaps you made a rash career or financial decision driven by emotions. Or maybe your feelings are ruling your decisions right now about living a healthy lifestyle. You don't *feel* like exercising or eating healthier. You *feel* like eating fast food every day, so you do.

I am not suggesting that feelings are wrong or that they should be ignored. Quite the opposite, in fact. I am saying that your emotions—and how you respond to them—shape your decisions for better or for worse.

They can lead you down the wrong path, keep you paralyzed with in-action, or propel you forward to success.

The root of the word *emotion* comes from the Latin verb *motere,* which means "to move." The prefix "e" suggests that the word literally means "to move away." Emotion, indeed, is all about motion. Our emotions conjure up impulses that "move" us, that make us want to take a particular action. Emotions such as anger, depression, insecurity, jealousy, and a sense of en-titlement can tempt you to behave in unhealthy ways.

On the other hand, understanding your emotions and what they're com-municating about your situation can serve as a tremendous boost toward achieving your potential. If you can unlock the messages behind your emo-tions, you will discover critical insights as to what is really holding you back. The chart on pages 64-66 details some of the emotions that can sabotage your success unless you pay attention to the messages they're sending. Which emotions characterize your feelings about your life and the specific circum-stances you face? What are they telling you? And how will you respond?

One of the most mature things you can do is identify your own fears, insecurities, and negative emotions and decide not to allow them to con-trol you. Instead, let your emotions awaken you to truths about yourself and guide you toward healthier responses to the challenges you encounter. Let me offer a few examples:

- If your significant other breaks off the relationship, and your response is to go shopping, you can acknowledge your own propensity to shop when you are upset. Recognize your sadness and hurt, then decide to process your grief in healthy ways, such as allowing yourself time to be sad, cry, or talk about your feelings with a trusted friend.

Emotion	Possible Message	Shaping Your Response
Anger	A boundary has been crossed.	What can I do to move on from my anger? What could I do differently to reduce the chance of this happening again?
Hopelessness	The things I want seem too far beyond my control. It's time to reprioritize and take action.	What's most important in my life? What can I do to honor that priority?
Sadness	I need to heal from whatever loss I've experienced.	It's healthy to mourn or to be sad for a time, but to be depressed is to remain stuck in that place. At what point will I choose to pick up the pieces and move forward?
Jealousy	I'd like to have more of a particular thing in my own life.	Decide to be content with your circumstances; determine whether your jealousy is a message that there is something missing in your life that you need to work on.
Entitlement	I believe I deserve more and better. Pride and ego are controlling my thoughts and decisions.	Where can I look for positive motivation?
Depression	I am dwelling on the most negative elements of my life.	What am I willing to do to take a positive step forward in my life? Despite the past, what do I want now from my life? *(Note: If depression lingers for more than a few weeks, it may indicate a more serious problem. Determine when and where to seek professional help.)*

Emotion	Possible Message	Shaping Your Response
Insecurity	I'm looking to things outside myself for confirmation of my value, worth, talents, and abilities.	I must reaffirm my value in God's eyes and refuse to judge myself by anyone's standards besides His, no matter how tempted I feel to do so.
Fear	I may be focused more on the potential for a negative outcome than on the potential for a positive outcome.	Preparation can help address my concerns. What else would help ease my fears? How could I reduce the risk that feeds my fear?
Shame	I am allowing past actions or experiences to define who I am.	What can I learn from this mistake or failure that will help me behave differently in the future?
Guilt	I have done something that is out of alignment with my values and beliefs.	Do I need to seek forgiveness from God, others, or myself? How can I ensure that I won't repeat this in the future?
Hurt	Others have failed to meet my expectations based on what I believe to be acceptable.	Do I need to revisit my standards, recognizing that others are only human and will inevitably do things that have the potential to hurt me? Am I prepared to choose not to take their mistakes, shortcomings, and failures personally?
Disappointment	I have set expectations for myself or others that were not met.	I must rethink my expectations.
Loneliness or Isolation	I have placed myself in an environment that does not encourage connection with others or perhaps even God.	How can I reconnect with others in meaningful relationships? When will I set aside time to engage in genuine, heartfelt communication with God?

Emotion	Possible Message	Shaping Your Response
Overloaded	My expectations of what I can accomplish in a given amount of time are too high.	Do I need to give myself more time, seek more help, narrow my priorities, or take on fewer responsibilities?
Overwhelmed	I've failed to take charge of my own schedule and have allowed circumstances and other people to determine my priorities.	What's most important to me? Am I willing to say no more often? What activities can I drop from my life to make room to focus on what's most important?
Resentment	I have allowed others to violate my boundaries, or my anger is misdirected.	What actions can I take to work through issues and conflicts rather than working around them and avoiding them?

- When you are feeling insecure, you can decide *not* to go out and spend money you don't have in order to impress others and make yourself feel more important. Instead, you can notice your past reactions. Then use your awareness of a potentially negative response and ask, "What could I do instead that would be more positive?"

- When a friend or family member buys that expensive new car or house, and you feel compelled to compete, remind yourself that you are too smart to dig deeper into debt just to satisfy emotions that are unhealthy.

- When you are angry and prone to say things you may later regret, notice how your emotions are threatening to negatively influence your words. Then choose to say nothing until you have calmed down.

- If you are afraid of failing in a relationship or afraid of being hurt, choose not to allow your emotions to stop you from opening yourself to the love you want in your life.

People who live based purely on how they feel never achieve their full potential. When we let our emotions take control, we feel frustrated, weak, and disappointed in ourselves. Many people are depressed simply because they continually make choices they are not proud of, that they don't feel good about, and that don't honor their values and beliefs.

For these reasons it's crucial that we not rely on emotions alone but allow our God-given intuition, knowledge, and wisdom to help guide our decisions. Remember, you can allow your feelings to control you, or you can make a decision to control your feelings. Sometimes you won't "feel" like doing what needs to be done, but mature people do what they know is right even when they don't feel like it. That is how you build character—and it is how you are able to grow into the person God created you to be.

Closing the Gap

Focus Your Thoughts
When strong emotions lead you in a particular direction, pause to think through what they're really telling you, and then choose your response carefully. Your awareness of the power of your feelings is the first step to ensuring that you will not make decisions that are blindly controlled by them.

Use Your Words Wisely
Set aside thirty minutes to journal about the emotions that rise to the surface when you think about the five key areas of your life—your relationships,

career, finances and resources, physical health and environments, and spiritual life. What do these emotions reveal about changes you need to make in your life?

Target Your Actions

Identify one action you've been hesitating to take because of negative emotions. Today, take that action.

Energize Your Spirit

Lord, Your Word says, "If [anyone] lacks wisdom, let him ask of God, who gives to all liberally and without reproach, and it will be given to him. But let him ask in faith, with no doubting, for he who doubts is like a wave of the sea driven and tossed by the wind"[James 1:5-6]. Today, I ask in faith that You would give me the wisdom to learn from my emotions and to use what I learn to break through my fears, obstacles, and misconceptions. Amen.

Ten

Are You Avoiding Pain or Embracing Joy?

Reconsider How You Make Your Decisions

Although he'd long planned to go back to school to obtain his MBA, Lee kept procrastinating. When I asked why, he said he was afraid that he wouldn't be accepted to graduate school. Even if he were accepted, he feared he might flunk out.

"What if you didn't get into graduate school?" I probed. "What then?"

"Well, I guess I wouldn't get my MBA," he replied matter-of-factly.

"And you don't have your MBA now, so you wouldn't be any worse off, right?"

"Right."

I pushed further. "I don't believe it will happen, but I'll ask you anyway. What if you failed out of graduate school?"

"Well, I'd be really embarrassed," he admitted.

"Anything else?"

"Umm. Let me think." He pondered for a moment. "No, that's it. I'd just be pretty embarrassed."

"Did you flunk out of college?" I asked, already knowing the answer.

"Well, no," he replied. "But I almost failed a couple of classes during college."

"So you didn't actually fail any classes in college?" I clarified.

"No."

"So basically, you're saying that you aren't applying to graduate school because you might not be accepted and because of the remote possibility that you might be embarrassed should you somehow flunk out?" I asked.

Our conversation helped Lee recognize that he was allowing fear to control his future, and he made a decision not to allow that fear to keep him from his heart's desire.

Whether we realize it or not, our decisions generally are guided by one of two motives: avoiding pain or embracing joy. When the fear of pain outweighs the perceived benefits of joy, we make choices based in fear. Understanding this basic dynamic can help you break free from the grip of fear. In Lee's case, what held him back was the potential for embarrassment if he failed, which was rather unlikely, based on his academic history. Just imagining the embarrassment was painful enough to prevent him from moving forward—until he realized what a small and unlikely hurdle that really was. Our fears are sometimes illusions, and we need to be willing to probe further until we uncover the truth about them. Then we need to ask, "What if my fears come true? What then?" Often you will be no worse off than if you had not attempted your goals at all. And even if you are worse off in some way, the attempt will still have been worth it.

Sadly, the actions of most people indicate that they are more interested in avoiding pain than in experiencing joy. They will go to great lengths to avoid pain and seem to view joy as only an indulgence. Yet our journey through life was intended to be filled with joy. This is not to say we won't endure painful experiences, but the fear of pain shouldn't be the guiding force in our decisions. Jesus provides the greatest example of the choice between avoiding pain or embracing joy: Hebrews 12:1-2 says, "Let us run with endurance the race that is set before us, looking unto Jesus, the author and finisher of our faith, who *for the joy that was set before Him* endured the cross, despising the shame, and has sat down at the right hand of the throne of God."

You may argue that you are motivated only by what God wants for you. Even so, when your love for God outweighs the temptation to base your choices on fear, insecurity, or pain, your motivation is the joy and fulfillment you experience through serving Him.

Many people live in fear, believing that joy is a luxury they can't afford. They haven't grasped the fact that joy comes from God and should be an underlying factor in every aspect of life. We are assured in the Old Testament that "the joy of the LORD is your strength" (Nehemiah 8:10). The writer of Ecclesiastes expressed it this way: "I know that there is nothing better for men than to be happy and do good while they live. That everyone may eat and drink, and find satisfaction in all his toil—this is the gift of God" (3:12-13, NIV).

We also know that joy is one fruit of the Spirit: "The fruit of the Spirit is love, *joy,* peace, longsuffering, kindness, goodness, faithfulness, gentleness, self-control. Against such there is no law" (Galatians 5:22-23).

So each of us who follows God is called to experience and produce joy in our life. To flee joy for the purpose of avoiding pain is to go against God's Word, which instructs us not to operate out of fear. Second Timothy 1:7

tells us, "God has not given us a spirit of fear, but of power and of love and of a sound mind." To make decisions out of fear is to throw away the power and sound mind God has given us. It means we lack the faith to stand firm in our purpose and destiny.

Joy, not fear, is God's will for your life.

Let's be careful, however, about how we define joy. I would suggest the following definition: Joy is an inner state of peace and thankfulness that embraces the goodness and grace God offers in every circumstance of life. You can find yourself in a challenging predicament and still experience joy in your soul. Joy is a state beyond happiness. Happiness is an emotion based on fleeting, positive circumstances. When those fleeting moments pass, so does happiness. But joy can remain through the trials and tribulations of life. Joy embraces every blessing, every gift, every opportunity. It delights in the ability to serve others and to experience God's love daily. Having joy is being thankful for every breath you draw, every friend you have made, and every chance you get to grow and do better in life.

I point this out because many decisions appear, from a worldly perspective, to embrace joy but are actually "pain avoidance" when viewed from a spiritual perspective. For example, if you engage in an extramarital affair, you may see it as "embracing joy" in your life and excuse your sin because it makes you happy—at least in the short term. But in truth, you entered into the affair as an escape from pain—perhaps the pain of frustration in your marriage, a midlife crisis, or low self-esteem that seems to improve with sexual attention. Likewise, if you aren't taking care of yourself and are feeling held back in your attempts to live a healthier lifestyle, you may feel that eating three big pieces of chocolate cake is about embracing joy because it tastes so delicious. However, in reality you are avoiding the pain of making a needed change. You know that God is pleased when you eat in moderation and take care of yourself, because your body is the temple of the Holy Spirit and, as such, should be treated extremely well.

After years of allowing the fear of pain to direct your life, it will take deliberate effort on your part to embrace joy. But I challenge you to reconsider how you make your decisions. Out of your commitment to doing what you are called to do and out of joy in accomplishing God's purposes for your life, you can endure any potential pain.

By becoming a living, breathing example of God's principles of love and fearlessness, you will gain the courage to break through all that is holding you back.

Closing the Gap

Focus Your Thoughts
Memorize this verse: "The joy of the LORD is your strength" (Nehemiah 8:10).

Use Your Words Wisely
Take five minutes to consider an important area of your life where you would like to make a change. Ask yourself these three questions, and write down your answers: What pain have I been avoiding by not making a needed change? In what ways would I feel differently about myself by making this change? What joy am I missing out on by not taking this step?

Target Your Actions
To get used to the idea of embracing joy, set aside thirty minutes to do something that brings you joy, such as spending time alone with God,

taking a walk in the park, soaking in a bubble bath, playing a round of golf, listening to your favorite album, or doing something that blesses someone else. Often, helping others is the greatest form of joy. Just remember not to neglect yourself in the process.

Energize Your Spirit

Dear God, I know I was not meant to spend my life trying to avoid pain. Help me to stop focusing on the potential for failure, rejection, and other painful consequences, and to instead focus on the joyful possibilities for living the life I was meant to live. I believe it is my responsibility to step over, around, or through my stumbling blocks. Give me the strength to do so consistently so that my life can serve as an example of Your love and power. Amen.

Eleven

What Are You Afraid Of?

Confront and Conquer Your Fears

Years ago, I visited Colorado Springs for a speaking engagement and a few meetings with my publisher—and learned an amusing lesson about the power of light to dissipate your fear. Steve, who works for my publishing company, and his wife picked me up from the airport. We headed to Glen Eyrie Castle and Conference Center, a Christian retreat center nestled in the foothills of the Rocky Mountains, near picturesque Pikes Peak. I had received a generous invitation from a staff member at Glen Eyrie to stay at no expense in a lovely room on the grounds, near a Tudor-style castle built by the Civil War general who founded Colorado Springs.

I'd been told the location was beautiful, but it was dark when we

Portions of this chapter are adapted from Valorie Burton's *Rich Minds, Rich Rewards* e-newsletter, May 12, 2004.

arrived. As we drove the gate onto the sprawling property, I began to feel a bit apprehensive. We followed a winding road with no street lights, and I could just make out a few small, dark cottages scattered here and there. The setting suggested to my active imagination the scene right before something crazy happens in a scary movie.

Just after 10 pm we pulled up to the building where I'd be staying. One light was on in the house, and I thought I saw a man sitting at a desk near a front window. We walked up to the oversize, ornate wooden door with a heavy metal knocker. Taped to the center of the door was a note with "Valorie" scribbled on the outside and a key inside, along with directions for finding my room inside this bed-and-breakfast-style cottage.

We walked through the foyer, then into a long, stately dining room with a fireplace and seating for fourteen. Next we came to a vast living area with portraits of people I imagined were long gone. As we proceeded through the dimly lit house, I thought, *Where am I? Who else is in this house? Are the former inhabitants still "with us"?* I knew I was being silly, but the thoughts and questions were gaining speed. At last we arrived at the door to my room—a spacious pink bedroom with a long, hall entry way, an antique canopy bed, living area, work area, and a huge bathroom. Steve saw the apprehension on my face. And his wife looked a little reluctant to leave me there.

"You don't have to stay here," he assured me. "We can go the Hilton right now if you want." I gazed through one of the dozen, ten-foot high windows in the room. It was pitch black outside so I couldn't see a thing. But I wasn't feeling excited about staying.

"It was such a generous offer that I would feel terrible about coming here and then leaving to check into a hotel," I said.

Just then, I heard a motherly voice call out, "Val-or-ie?" Moments later a lovely, older couple —the home's hosts—entered the room.

The husband, perhaps sensing a little tension by the way we were scoping out the room, said lightly, "Don't worry. There are no ghosts here. It just looks like this because you came at night."

A little embarrassed, I said, "Oh, I'm sure it's lovely in the daytime, hoping I was right.

The host's wife proceeded to tell me a few things about the room and the house. She said something about an unconventional wake-up call at 5:30 am, but I thought she was kidding. "Good night," they said before retiring to their room.

"Well," I said to Steve and his wife. "I'll stay tonight and let's see how it goes."

"I'll be back to pick you up in the morning," he offered. "Just pack your bags if you want to check into a hotel tomorrow, and we'll take them when I pick you up."

I readied for bed while firmly telling myself that my fear was unfounded. Nevertheless, I left the hallway light on for good measure.

Around 5:20 am, I awoke to the sound of a woman laughing— well, kind of cackling. It was almost a giggle—little short, choppy bursts of laughter. The first time I heard it, I thought it was a bit strange. The second time, I thought, B*oy, something must really be funny.* I tried to go back to sleep, but those funny little giggles continued. W*hat could be that funny this early in the morning?* Now I was feeling a bit annoyed.

Then I remembered the hostess's warning that I would get a wake-up call around 5:30 in the morning. I jumped out of bed and looked outside. Huge, wild, black turkeys were shuffling about on the lawn and gobbling contentedly. In the background was a spectacular mountain view, and I could see the edges of a large, stone castle peeking from behind the tall, evergreen trees on the property. The twelve expansive windows in my room looked out on a captivating scene. I took a deep breath of gratitude and inhaled the beauty of nature. Then I laughed at myself for my reaction the night before.

During my three days at Glen Eyrie I took walks, meditated, and soaked in the scenic, peaceful environment.

And I gleaned a simple lesson from this experience: Sometimes, you have to persevere through the fear that comes in darkness to experience the beautiful vision that comes with the dawning of light. Things aren't always as they seem, especially when we have a limited view.

In what area of your life are you afraid because you can't see what's coming? Are you ready to bail out quickly before you can see the whole picture? Refuse to allow irrational fears to pressure you into making hasty decisions—whether in your personal or professional life. "Weeping may endure for a night, but joy comes in the morning," Psalm 30:5 promises. Stick around and see what God has in store before you take it upon yourself to "fix things" out of fear. When you finally see what morning looks like, you may just find you were in the right place all along.

In what way are you tempted to make a premature decision? Is God prompting you to wait a little while longer before showing you the bigger picture? Be patient. Refuse to make a hasty decision. Instead, endure a little discomfort until you can see the bigger picture and make a more informed decision.

In what areas of your life is fear holding you back? Perhaps you're tempted to run away from or ignore the mountain of debt that stands between you and your goal of financial health and prosperity. Maybe a healthy long-term relationship is just a few steps away, but your fear of commitment sends you running in the other direction. Are negative voices convincing you that you lack the necessary skills to achieve your career or business goals?

Whatever is keeping you from an important personal goal right now, I challenge you to regain your composure and take a few steps forward. Fear, as you may have heard before, is just an acronym for "False Evidence Appearing Real." You fear what you think *might* happen, which is often based on irrational thought, misinformation, or misconceptions.

For example, Joyce, one of my coaching clients, was plugging along in her business, successful but not immensely so. She was a talented graphic artist, and her work spoke for itself. Referrals from existing clients were steady, so she always had business. Still, another level of opportunity had gone completely untapped.

When I asked what was really holding her back, Joyce said that she loved her work but was terrified of "selling" it. "I'm so afraid of the rejection that is inevitable when you have to ask people for their business. I feel like I'm intruding on them."

The fear, based not on fact or experience but solely on irrational thought, was so strong that Joyce had been in business for four years without ever actively selling her services. In fact, she was afraid to call prospective clients when colleagues referred them to her; she always waited for others to approach her. There was one potential client, in particular, with whom she really wanted to work, but she was afraid to make a phone call to introduce herself and her business.

Via telephone we spent a coaching session outlining her strategy, and she agreed to make the call as soon as our session ended, when her confidence and momentum would be the highest.

After we hung up, Joyce stared at the phone for five minutes before picking it up again, and she rehearsed aloud what she would say when her potential client answered the phone. Fearful thoughts and emotions were racing through her mind: *What if I freeze? What if she's aggravated that I called? What if she doesn't need my services? I'll just be bothering her and wasting her time.*

Though her heart was racing and her palms were sweaty, Joyce determined not to let her fear stop her. As she described it, she took advantage of a sudden rush of confidence after saying aloud, "I'm great at what I do, and I'll be doing her a service to let her know that I'm available to help with her graphics needs." Joyce dialed the number quickly before the negative thoughts could rush back in. The phone began to ring. No answer. Voice mail picked up. She looked at the bullet points from her script, left a short message, and hung up. To her delight, the prospective client called back the same day and said that their mutual acquaintance had mentioned Joyce's talent. They scheduled a meeting for a week later. Joyce's portfolio was a hit, and the prospective client became a new client—her largest account to date!

Joyce was able to identify her problem as a fear of rejection, but some people find it difficult to pinpoint their fear because it's a common thread woven through every single aspect of their life. Whatever the topic, challenge, or opportunity, their response stems from a spirit of fear. They've allowed fear to control them for so long that it's taken over their life.

Whatever the level of fear in your life, the secret to confronting and conquering it is to be honest and direct. Ask yourself "What if?" questions:

- "What if I am successful and people criticize me?"

- "What if I take a leap of faith and start a business, and then it fails?"
- "What if people reject me and say no?"

Identifying your fear and answering your "What if?" questions helps you see that life will still go on even if your worst fear becomes reality. It also gives you the opportunity to plan a safety net that will reduce your risk and decrease your fear.

One of my clients recently mentioned a job she'd love to have, but she didn't think she should apply for it because she had not completed her bachelor's degree. Given her thirty years of professional experience, I told her she was more than qualified and asked her what was the worst thing that could happen if she applied. "I might not get the job," she replied, "and I could handle that."

Overcoming your fears requires you to ask "What if?" and then decide how to handle the possible outcomes ahead of time.

Even with advance preparation and planning, we can still be caught off guard by our fears. The fact is, you are human, and you will sometimes overreact to a situation. At the same time, these reactions are behaviors you have practiced for a lifetime; you can choose to practice new behaviors. You do not have to allow your first reaction to be your permanent response. Reactions do not tap into your wisdom, spiritual discernment, or rational thought. Responses, however, tap into all three.

In order to break free from what's holding you back, you must deliberately choose to respond to the adverse and intimidating circumstances of life rather than simply react to them. Whatever you have been running away from, make a decision today to change your mind and, thus, your response.

Closing the Gap

Focus Your Thoughts

Memorize this verse: "God has not given us a spirit of fear, but of power and of love and of a sound mind" (2 Timothy 1:7).

Use Your Words Wisely

When fearful thoughts come into your mind, counter them with truth. Write out empowering, truthful statements and scriptures, and post them in places where you will see them regularly. Recite them aloud when you need an extra dose of confidence.

Target Your Actions

Pinpoint your most pressing fears. Then ask yourself, "What if this fear actually came true? What then?" Being able to identify the consequences that might occur if your fear became reality gives you the power to see your fear at face value. Next, ask yourself, "What would it take for me to reduce my fear?" Take action to make your fear less intimidating.

Energize Your Spirit

God, help me to be mindful of my fears and notice my automatic reactions so that I can regain my composure and try a new response. Throughout the Bible You instruct Your people to be strong and of good courage. Help me to be strong in the face of my fears and to be courageous in following You as You lead me to respond in ways I never have before. Amen.

Twelve

What Do You Really Believe?

Reject the Lies That Hold You Back

E rin was just a year out of graduate school when an interesting position opened in her company. She knew she could do the job well, but she didn't believe she would be given a fair shot at the promotion.

Her mother, a sharp and intelligent woman, had experienced both racism and sexism throughout her career, and she had warned her daughter against getting her hopes up about achieving her career goals. "Don't expect to be treated fairly, Erin," her mother had warned. "You're a woman *and* a minority. That's two strikes against you."

Throughout her childhood, Erin had witnessed the ordeals her mother endured—being more qualified, working harder, and having a better track record than her colleagues, yet repeatedly being passed over for the best assignments. Her mother's experience had shaped Erin's beliefs and left her convinced that no matter what she did, she would face the same struggles in the workplace.

Unfortunately, Erin's beliefs showed up in subtle ways at work, prompting her to be defensive and suspicious of her co-workers and supervisors. As a result, she was unable to connect in a meaningful way with the people who could best influence her chances for success. She lost out on the promotion, not for the reasons she believed, but because her beliefs fed a negative attitude, and that attitude led to actions that were counterproductive to her vision for her career.

In chapter 9 I talked about the importance of paying attention to the messages your emotions are sending you. Your emotions and automatic reactions to certain situations are born of your personal experiences, dating back to childhood. The majority of our beliefs are formed before we become adults, and they tend to stick with us for life. This isn't necessarily a problem unless those beliefs are unhealthy or have been skewed by negative experiences or influences.

For example, one of my coaching clients, Jennifer, felt that success would always elude her. Throughout her childhood and teen years, her family members had consistently undermined her confidence and self-esteem. She had endured verbally abusive insults, and her own parents frequently reminded her that she'd never amount to much. Decades later, as those evil lies echoed in her mind, Jennifer didn't even put up a fight. She simply let them play over and over again, feeling like a wounded little girl, helpless once again to defend herself against her family's cruel words.

"What are you really afraid of?" I asked as we discussed growing her business.

"I'm afraid they were right," she said. "I feel like a fraud at times, like I'm really not good enough to be doing what I do, and if I keep pushing ahead, someone is going to find me out."

Not surprisingly, Jennifer's low self-esteem had affected more than her business; it also influenced how she approached her relationships and her finances. She settled for less than she deserved in her relationships. She sought to raise her worth through material possessions—to the point of extreme financial strain.

Her first step in conquering the lies that were holding her back involved becoming aware of her present-moment thoughts as she moved forward in her business. We focused on countering the voice of the Enemy with words of truth. I asked specific questions to help her counter her own negative thoughts and misperceptions.

"What indicates that you're not good enough?" I asked. To her delight she was unable to come up with one answer to that question.

"What indicates that you are good enough and capable of owning a prosperous business?" I asked. Again, to her delight Jennifer began to list a string of character traits—perseverance, creativity, intelligence, personality, passion—that indicated she had just what she needed to succeed, despite what anyone else might think. Just hearing herself list her positive traits was a powerful exercise in countering her false thought patterns.

Like many of us, Jennifer was held back by false beliefs. Sadly, the seeds of her distress were planted by those who should have been nurturing her hopes and dreams. Few parents, thankfully, are as heartless as Jennifer's were. Most do their best to raise emotionally healthy children, yet it is quite common for those same children to enter the adult world not truly believing in their potential and possibilities.

This is, at least in part, because the media and other sources have bombarded us with messages that are contrary to the Word of God. Peers, teachers, and others may have pointed out your flaws and limitations rather than directing your attention to the truth that you are "fearfully and wonderfully" made (Psalm 139:14). You may have been discouraged from dreaming big, taught to protect your heart from disappointment, even though the Bible declares, "With God *all* things are possible" (Matthew 19:26). The world urges you to hate your enemies and seek revenge. Jesus tells you to "love your enemies, bless those who curse you, do good to those who hate you, and pray for those who spitefully use you and persecute you" (Matthew 5:44).

Whether or not you realize it, you have most likely bought into one or more of these lies, or others like them. And these mistaken beliefs are holding you back in ways you may not have noticed.

While you may verbally affirm your belief in God's power and compassion, your daily decisions—and your ability to move toward your vision—will be guided by what you *really* believe. If a hidden camera recorded your daily interactions, what would the footage reveal about your belief in God's Word? Would your words and actions reveal a wholehearted trust in God? Would your behavior toward others demonstrate a loving attitude? Would your response to obstacles and challenges confirm that you realize you don't have to do everything in your own strength?

"Faith without works is dead," the Bible tells us (James 2:26). In part this means you must act on what you know to be true according to the Word of God. The only way to overcome the inevitable obstacles in your life is to believe in and claim the promises of God for yourself. Despite whatever your past negative experiences and associations may have led you to be believe, you must be willing to align your actions with your faith.

Begin to question the things you believe that may be counterproductive to achieving your vision and fulfilling God's purposes for your life. Notice what your words, attitudes, and actions indicate regarding your beliefs about money, the opposite sex, time, marriage, and people in general.

Reject the lies that are holding you back, and embrace the truths of your unchangeable, loving God.

Closing the Gap

Focus Your Thoughts

Meditate on these words: "Whatever things you ask in prayer, believing, you will receive" (Matthew 21:22).

Use Your Words Wisely

Examine your attitudes, words, and actions, and ask yourself what they reveal about your beliefs and any lies that have taken root in your life. Write down all the answers that come to mind, and explore the ways these beliefs have kept you from success in the past.

Target Your Actions

Be alert today for anything that indicates your decisions are being guided by worldly wisdom rather than God's wisdom. Then counter your initial response with one that is aligned with truth.

Energize Your Spirit

Lord, today I claim for myself Your promise to supply all my needs (Philippians 4:19). I choose to trust in Your love and faithfulness, and I ask You to cleanse from my mind any lies that threaten to undermine my faith. Please guide my daily decisions so that they will be aligned with the truths of Your Word. Amen.

Thirteen

Are You Waiting for Perfect Circumstances?

Trust God to Overcome Your Limitations

Did you know that Moses, one of the greatest people in the Old Testament, initially resisted God's call to lead the Israelites out of slavery? You might think that when God speaks directly to a person out of a burning bush, he or she would be impressed with the importance of the situation and rush off to complete any instructions given. Not so with Moses. He kept pointing out the challenges that might stand in the way of success.

First, he worried that his own people wouldn't take him seriously: "What if they do not believe me or listen to me and say, 'The LORD did not appear to you'?" (Exodus 4:1, NIV). In response to this concern, God equipped Moses to perform wondrous signs that would erase any doubt that God had sent him.

Still, Moses had reservations about his chances for success:

> Moses said to the LORD, "O Lord, I have never been eloquent,
> neither in the past nor since you have spoken to your servant. I am
> slow of speech and tongue."
>
> The LORD said to him, "Who gave man his mouth? Who
> makes him deaf or mute? Who gives him sight or makes him blind?
> Is it not I, the LORD? Now go; I will help you speak and will teach
> you what to say." (Exodus 4:10-12, NIV)

Isn't that awesome? God empathized with Moses's insecurity about his speech impediment, a serious imperfection in Moses's opinion. But God didn't accept it as an excuse for evading his assigned mission. Instead, He promised to teach Moses just what to say and to help him speak.

Amazingly, even God's assurance of divine help was not enough to quell Moses's doubts. Moses replied: "O Lord, please send someone else to do it" (Exodus 4:13, NIV).

As you might expect, God was frustrated, even angered by Moses's lack of faith.

> Then the LORD's anger burned against Moses and he said,
> "What about your brother, Aaron the Levite? I know he can
> speak well. He is already on his way to meet you, and his heart
> will be glad when he sees you. You shall speak to him and put
> words in his mouth; I will help both of you speak and will teach
> you what to do. He will speak to the people for you, and it will
> be as if he were your mouth and as if you were God to him."
> (Exodus 4:14-16, NIV)

Despite Moses's lack of faith, our compassionate God provided an alternative so that he did not have to speak. God worked through him and around his fear simultaneously!

As you know, Moses finally moved forward to complete his assignment and began exercising what little faith he had. God used him to change the course of history. And as his faith grew, Moses moved past his fears and insecurities and trusted God to fill the gaps in his leadership abilities.

Most of us can relate to Moses's concerns about his imperfect circumstances. We hesitate to move forward even when the way ahead is clearly marked, because we are convinced we don't have what it takes to succeed. We focus on our own shortcomings or the limitations of our circumstances rather than looking to God to make a way. Like Moses, we may even beg God to provide an alternative, to let us off the hook so we won't have to risk failure. Although God has promised to be with us wherever we go, we may doubt His ability—or willingness—to come through in our moment of need. Let me suggest that doubting God is generally a bad idea. As with Moses, He can get frustrated when we argue with Him. He has already promised that all things are possible with Him; what further assurance do we need?

I am convinced that most often we are held back by excuses that really don't measure up to their claims:

- "I would eat healthier, but I don't have time to cook."
- "I would love to go back to school, but I'll wait until my schedule slows down."
- "We can't take a vacation right now. We have too much to do."
- "I'm not ready to start my business yet. I need to finish my business plan."

- "I wish I had more time with my family, but work demands are just too high right now."

The truth is, if you want something badly enough, you won't make excuses about why it cannot be done. You'll clear your calendar for the right goal. If you really want to start eating healthier, you will find a way. When you are truly driven to start that business, you'll do whatever it takes to get it off the ground.

When you find yourself postponing an action you need to take because you're waiting for perfect circumstances, it's time to either question your behavior (so what's *really* holding me back?) or take action. Perfect circumstances are extremely rare. Yes, at times it will seem that events in your life have been divinely orchestrated and things couldn't have worked out more perfectly. But most likely you'll only notice that in retrospect. Generally, as we look at the path ahead, rather than smooth pavement we will see an obstacle course of speed bumps, potholes, and detours. At these times we can find encouragement in Romans 8:28: "We know that all things work together for good to those who love God, to those who are the called according to His purpose."

You'll never move forward if you are waiting for "perfection" that *you* can see rather than trusting that God sees perfection where you see only the problems. The Lord told the apostle Paul, "My grace is sufficient for you, for My strength is made perfect in weakness" (2 Corinthians 12:9).

God is at work in imperfect circumstances. He will take your limitations, shortcomings, and flaws and create opportunities and situations that are perfectly aligned with where you need to be and what you need to learn at given points in your life.

It would certainly be easier to step forward if we knew that everything was lined up perfectly, but who needs faith to do that? When we cannot anticipate exactly what's going to happen next, when circumstances appear imperfect, when we feel weak, only then can our faith truly be tested. It's normal to be afraid when you step out of your comfort zone, but as Moses learned, each victory will increase your faith. As you move forward despite your fears, you'll experience a sense of accomplishment that will serve to strengthen your trust in God.

Stop waiting on perfect circumstances! The time to take action is now.

Closing the Gap

Focus Your Thoughts
Read Philippians 4:11-13. Consider the potential challenges you will face in moving forward. Can you say in faith with Paul, "I can do all things through Christ who strengthens me"?

Use Your Words Wisely
Ask yourself, "In what situation am I waiting on perfect circumstances before I take action?" Explore your answer in your journal. Turn back to chapter 8 for questions that will help you dig below the surface and discover the source of your hesitation.

Target Your Actions
Using the information you learned in the previous exercise, identify one step you can take to move toward your goals this week. Then take it!

Energize Your Spirit

Dear God, I ask You to empower me to move forward despite my insecurities, limited experience, or any other circumstance I might deem "imperfect." Thank You that Your strength is made perfect in my weakness. May You receive all the glory as I succeed on my journey in spite of my weaknesses and challenges. Amen.

Fourteen

Have You Given Away Your Power?

Accept Responsibility for Your Choices

I watched in disbelief in the grocery store one day as a four-year-old bossed his mother around. "I want this!" the obnoxious little guy barked at his mother.

"Okay, honey, you can have it, but please don't yell at Mommy," she replied nervously, seeming embarrassed that anyone else could hear the conversation.

"I'm ready to go! Let's go!" he demanded a minute later.

"Mommy has a couple more items on the list before we'll be finished, okay?" She seemed to be apologizing.

The child's demanding whine echoed throughout the store: "I want to go! I want to go!"

The mother rushed through the store, talking to her son the whole time. "We're almost finished. Please just be patient," she begged repeatedly in a hushed tone. "Don't yell now, you're making too much noise." As I stood behind them at the checkout, I overheard her say to the cashier that she couldn't finish her list because "when he's ready to go, I just can't get my shopping done."

Have you ever noticed that some children don't ask their parents' permission for anything? They just do as they please. *No* isn't a word they easily understand. I'm always amazed when I observe this sort of behavior. As a child I was no paragon of virtue, but I was raised to respect and obey not only my parents but every adult in our family. I learned at an early age that not everything I wanted would automatically be granted; I had to seek permission from a higher authority. If I wanted to go outside, I asked permission. If I wanted to leave the dinner table, I asked to be excused. If I was ready to leave a store early, well, it didn't really matter because I was not in charge.

Some of the things that keep us from moving toward our vision can be compared to unruly children whom we've allowed to rule our lives. We've convinced ourselves that whatever is holding us back is beyond our control, when in truth we've simply relinquished our power, allowing situations, fears, people, misconceptions, or painful emotions to take control of our choices.

For example, if someone betrays your trust, you might wallow in misery for a while, feeling sorry for yourself. You might decide never to trust anyone again. You might even choose to believe that you are unworthy of being treated any better. You might convince yourself that the betrayer forced you into these behaviors. However, the truth is that you are in control. All these reactions are temptations, choices you can take or leave. Yes, the other person may have left you feeling wounded and angry, but only you can give those feelings permission to shape your actions and attitudes.

It's time to recognize that whatever is holding you back has your permission to do so. Unless God is restraining you for a purpose, nothing can hold you back without your consent. Fear needs your permission to control your actions. Anger needs permission to be translated into words or actions. A pity party needs permission to pitch a tent in your mind.

Often the things we give permission to hold us back are nothing more than excuses in disguise. Rather than looking beneath the surface of our circumstances, we state the obvious as the reason we've made little progress. "I'm too busy" or "I don't have enough money" or "They won't let me." We blame our childhood traumas, gender, racial or ethnic background, lack of education, and even other people. Of course the circumstances of our lives will present hurdles from time to time. But those hurdles only become roadblocks when we allow them to take over. If, on the other hand, we view them as challenges, even opportunities, we are on our way to regaining control of our lives.

For example, during a Q and A session at one of my book signings, a woman declared, "Life dictates my schedule, so I just cannot find the time to spend alone that you recommend." What do you think? Was she being honest with herself?

The truth is that we create our own schedules, whether purposefully or subconsciously. Life does not dictate your schedule. You choose it. Now some choices may have greater consequences than others, but they are your choices nonetheless. For example, in order to free up some time in your schedule, you can choose not to go to work tomorrow. You may not have a job the next day, but the choice is yours to make. A healthier approach might be to choose to show up for work but confront your need for change. You might ask yourself, "What could I do to create a schedule that serves my priorities and vision? Where am I 'wasting' my time—watching television, surfing the Internet, going to the movies—when I could be investing time in my priorities? To whom can I turn for help in dealing with some of my lower-priority responsibilities so that I will have more time to pursue my vision?" A new schedule may not evolve overnight, but it is within your power to make the changes you want.

It's often easier to make excuses than to accept responsibility for being stuck, but you have the ability, if you so desire, to let go of your excuses and face the truth about your options.

Make a list of the five biggest problems you're facing today. Then, after praying and looking honestly at your life, make a check mark in the appropriate column to indicate whether that problem is an excuse you need to confront or a hurdle you can overcome.

Problem	Excuse	Hurdle

Our lives are the sum total of our choices. The decisions you make daily cause you to close the gap between where you are and where God wants you to be, maintain the gap, or widen it. God has given you free will, but if you want to gain ground rather than lose it, you must choose not to relinquish your power to situations, fears, people, misconceptions, or painful emotions. Remember, nothing can hold you back without your permission. Learn to say no to the excuses and to accept responsibility for your choices.

Closing the Gap

Focus Your Thoughts

When counterproductive, condemning, or fearful thoughts enter your mind, fight them with positive truths. Romans 12:2 tells us, "Do not conform any longer to the pattern of this world, but be transformed by the renewing of your mind" (NIV). You may not choose the thoughts that enter your mind, but you can choose which ones you allow to stay there.

Use Your Words Wisely

Listen carefully to your own words during the next forty-eight hours. Be on the lookout for phrases that indicate you've given away your power; then think of ways to restate your decision. For example, if you find yourself saying "I can't" in a particular situation, you can turn that around by saying, "I choose to" or "I choose not to because…"

Target Your Actions

The people you choose to spend time with can have a great impact on your attitude toward life. Consider which of your friends most invigorates and encourages you; then treat that person to lunch or coffee. Be sure not to use your time as an opportunity to complain, but instead practice couching your words in positive terms.

Energize Your Spirit

In the name of Jesus, I declare that no invisible force has control over my life, my actions, or my decisions without my consent. Lord, help me to walk boldly in this knowledge and, with the guidance of Your Holy Spirit, to take charge of my life! Amen.

Fifteen

Are You Working Around Problems or Working Through Them?

Break the Cycle of Unhealthy Behavior

For years Kelly's parents had practiced healthy financial habits. Their commitment to living below their means and saving 20 percent of their income had laid the foundation for solid financial security. But somehow Traci and John had failed to instill their financial values in Kelly. Now thirty-five years old, single, and earning an above-average salary—more than $60,000 annually—Kelly seemed unable to get her finances in order. Her parents frequently came to her rescue, bailing her out of the problems that arose from her irresponsibility.

She explained to me that while she didn't feel good about accepting money from her parents on a regular basis, she needed the money to stay afloat. Besides, she reasoned, they seemed to enjoy helping her out. "It makes them feel like they're still needed," she said.

"And how does it make you feel?" I asked.

"Like a real failure," she admitted. "I'm ashamed of the financial mess I've made and of the fact that my parents have to come to my rescue. I should be able to take care of myself, but I never have."

Both Kelly and her parents were being held back from success in the area of relationships and finances. An ongoing pattern of emotional spending on Kelly's part and needy parenting on Traci and John's part created an unhealthy cycle of mutual dependence. Until all three of them seek to address the underlying issues, the cycle will continue. Unless Traci and John address their need to be needed, they will have no real motivation for helping Kelly address her poor financial health. If Kelly fails to explore why she has been living above her means her entire adult life and refuses to stop doing so, she will continue to be dependent upon her parents for financial survival.

As with this family, many people perpetuate their own problems by failing to tackle them head-on. They tiptoe around the edge of the issue, tweaking things here and there but never fully confronting the problem, either because they aren't ready to face the truth about themselves or because they're trying to avoid conflict with those around them.

Here are a few examples of working around a problem rather than working through it:

- You "solve" your financial dilemmas by continually borrowing money, running up credit-card debt, or avoiding creditors.
- You look to pills, fad diets, or other quick fixes to lose weight so that you don't have to exercise or change your eating habits.
- You avoid difficult conversations or pretend you are not angry or upset when really you are.

- You pretend to be happy, though you can't remember the last time you felt true joy.
- You buy things for your children or spouse out of guilt for things you've done (or haven't done).
- You do things out of habit or tradition even when they've lost their meaning for you.
- You pursue a divorce without exhausting all avenues of saving your marriage.
- You bounce from job to job, church to church, or relationship to relationship in search of a setting that will meet your needs.

It takes a great deal of energy to avoid issues, to pretend everything is fine, and to continually seek substitutes for peace, joy, and truth. When you work around your problems instead of working through them, it's like running around your home to swat each individual fly, wasp, or mosquito instead of repairing the gaping hole in the window screen. It's exhausting…and almost pointless. Eventually you may just decide to live with the pests, reasoning that they'll never go away entirely, so why waste your effort.

Until you stop working around problems and start working through them, you will find yourself indefinitely stuck, enduring a less-than-fulfilling situation. However, with God directing your steps, you can step out in faith to break your cycle of unresolved problems.

Begin by considering specific situations that seem to recur in your life. Is money an ongoing problem? How about a particular topic or attitude that always results in conflict with a loved one? Is there an opportunity you are trying to force to happen, to no avail? Be truthful with yourself and try the following:

1. Admit the problem, and don't be afraid to deal with it.

2. Identify your options for eliminating the recurring problem.
3. Make a radical change, if needed, applying the tools you're gaining from this book.

It can be difficult to admit that you need to put a stop to an ongoing problem. Maintaining the status quo means staying within your comfort zone, not having to face the truth or make difficult changes.

But if you're serious about closing the gap and moving toward your most fulfilling life, it's time to break the cycle of unhealthy behavior and tackle those problems directly.

Closing the Gap

Focus Your Thoughts
When you find yourself dwelling on a recurring problem, refocus your thoughts on a solution. Ask yourself, "What will I need to do to keep this problem from plaguing my life in the future?"

Use Your Words Wisely
When problems or conflicts arise today, don't simply seek to smooth things over. Instead, face the issue head-on and ask, "What's this really about? And how can I work through it or resolve it?"

Target Your Actions
Identify one repetitive problem in your life, and make a decision about what you could do to work through it. If you feel stuck, seek help through prayer and Bible study, or speak with a wise and trusted friend, coach, or advisor.

Energize Your Spirit
Lord, please help me notice when I am tiptoeing around problems. Then give me the strength, courage, and wisdom to deal with the problems directly and work through them honestly and effectively. Amen.

Sixteen

What Habits Do You Need to Replace?

Condition Yourself to Respond in Positive Ways

S teven Jehu, a seventeen-year-old British gymnast, had just returned to his hotel after a training session for the European Gymnastics Championship in Slovenia in April 2004. As he leaned out of an open window, the safety bar unexpectedly gave way, sending Jehu plunging from the fourth floor. The quick-thinking athlete, whose mind and body were conditioned for flying through the air, responded by doing a midair somersault and landing on his feet. As a result, this medal-winning gymnast suffered only a broken ankle and a few minor injuries from his potentially fatal thirty-three-foot fall.

Portions of this chapter are adapted from Valorie Burton's *Rich Minds, Rich Rewards* e-newsletter, September 30, 2004.

Whether or not we realize it, each of us is conditioned, through years of building habits both deliberate and unconscious, to respond automatically when confronted with challenging situations. Sadly, many people are conditioned to respond with fear or anger rather than with the unruffled confidence displayed by Steven Jehu.

Back in chapter 7 we identified some of the issues that may be creating roadblocks on your journey toward fulfillment. Each of these restraints is both reflected in and reinforced by self-sabotaging habits, practices that affect your decisions each day. These negative thoughts and actions yield dissatisfying results that serve to underscore your fears—and perpetuate the cycle of defeat.

As mentioned earlier, most of us are held back by just a few key issues that manifest themselves in any number of bad habits. If you can replace these habits, you will dramatically change the results you've been getting. Once you've identified the habits that are perpetuating your negative responses, you can begin the process of reconditioning—eliminating and replacing them with positive, healthy habits.

Let's take a closer look at the habits that accompany and sustain the most common underlying issues. As you read through the chart on pages 104-106, circle or highlight each attitude, thought pattern, or action you recognize as part of your conditioned response to challenges. Then note the reconditioned habits you can adopt to help conquer your fears and obstacles.

Personal transformation often begins with one small adjustment that opens the way for massive change. Small but meaningful changes teach us to exercise self-control and empower us to take action in multiple areas. For example, if your relationship with a particular family member is fraught with tension, you might decide that you will no longer engage in arguments with him. Each time he says something that pushes your buttons, you determine

Issue	*Perpetuating Habits*	*Reconditioned Habits*
Fear of failure	Unwillingness to try; perfectionism; procrastination	Willingness to risk failure; giving up the need to be perfect or do things perfectly; taking action
Fear of success	Eagerness to blame others when things go wrong; procrastination	Accepting responsibility for the outcome of your efforts; refusing to blame or make excuses for failure; accepting the new responsibilities of success
Fear of rejection	Hesitation to ask for what you want; tendency to shrink from who you really are; procrastination; inclination to make excuses	Separating rejection of your requests or ideas from rejection of you as a person; refusing to lose your enthusiasm; accepting rejection as a normal process on the road to success
Fear of inadequacy	Criticism of others; overcompensation for insecurities; overspending; tendency to place others on a pedestal; unreasonably hard on yourself	Acknowledging your positive attributes and progress; focusing on being good to yourself; resisting the temptation to compare yourself to others; loving yourself unconditionally; accepting God's unconditional love for you
Laziness	Acceptance of mediocrity; willingness to live without goals or a game plan; procrastination; tolerance for just getting by; inclination to make excuses	Working hard; pursuing goals that inspire you; practicing self-discipline (one "fruit of the Spirit" from Galatians 5:22-23)
Pride	Arrogance; intolerance of others' issues and weaknesses; judgmental attitude	Allowing no room for your ego; practicing humility and compassion
Pessimism	Negative talk; tendency to believe the worst; lack of faith	Exhibiting a positive, hopeful attitude; choosing optimism; trusting God

Issue	Perpetuating Habits	Reconditioned Habits
Negativity	Inclination to talk down about nearly everyone and everything; lack of enthusiasm; attitude that drains your own energy as well as that of others; inability to enjoy life	Refusing to dwell on problems or to talk negatively about others, murmur, or complain; enjoying the little things in life
Lack of purpose	Poor choices; willingness to follow others' guidance rather than seeking your own path	Purposeful decision making; respect for your own gifts, talents, and experiences
Lack of focus	Easily distracted; poor discipline; weak commitment to projects and goals	Practicing disciplined daily habits
Lack of personal growth	Failure to draw lessons from experiences; repetition of mistakes in different situations; resistance to change	Flexibility; learning lessons from your mistakes, failures, and experiences; willingness to change so you can grow
Lack of spiritual growth	Weak or nonexistent relationship with God; disobedience; failure to act upon God's clear leading; refusal to trust God	Prayer; daily communication with God; seeking the lesson in your circumstances and experiences; trusting God
Lack of faith	Tendency to remain stuck in place; complacency; disobedience; failure to act upon God's clear leading; refusal to trust God; attempt to accomplish everything on your own	Taking leaps of faith; dreaming a bigger vision; acting on God's promptings; relying on God's supernatural strength
Need for approval	Inclination to say yes when the answer should be no; overcommitment; allowing others to violate boundaries or take advantage; going along with the status quo; failure to confront disrespectful behavior; overachievement; tendency to talk too much	Saying yes only when you really mean it; learning to say no to requests that do not fit your purpose and priorities; standing up for yourself; not trying to win others' approval

Issue	Perpetuating Habits	Reconditioned Habits
Complacency	Acceptance of less than is deserved; disregard for your talent and passion	Excellence; passion
Guilt	Inability to forgive yourself for past mistakes; overcompensation for perceived failures or inadequacies; unhealthy or poor decisions; eagerness to blame others or to point out their flaws; inclination to make excuses	Accepting God's forgiveness and mercy; forgiving yourself
Shame	Suppression of your true self; inability to forgive yourself; resistance to pursuing your dreams	Forgiving yourself; accepting God's grace and mercy; freeing yourself to press forward rather than focusing on your past
Avoidance	Failure to confront people, issues, and challenges as needed; tendency not to speak up or express true feelings	Employing truthfulness and boldness with yourself and others; refusing to "work around" problems

to respond peacefully or not at all. Incorporating that one change in that one relationship will strengthen your self-control and help you gain the experience and confidence to make similar changes in other relationships.

In addition, making a commitment to short-term change can build momentum for a long-term change. A few years ago a colleague who had been a smoker for more than twenty years decided to cut out cigarettes for one week. Buoyed by his success, he decided to see how long he could abstain. One week turned into a month and then a year. Today he's still smoke-free.

I challenge you to incorporate into your life one small but meaningful change for the next seven consecutive days. Seven days is long enough to "try out" the change, prove to yourself that you can do it, and experience the difference it makes. You can do anything for seven days, right? Think for a moment about one of the restraints in your life. What change would address the source of the issue and set you free? Here are a few ideas:

Bad Habit	*Reconditioned Habit*	*Seven-Day Change*
Procrastination	Meeting deadlines consistently	Spend thirty minutes each day taking action toward a key goal
Unhealthy eating	Making wise food choices	Eliminate red meat, junk food, or caffeine from your diet
Running behind schedule	Being someone others can rely on	Be ten minutes early for every appointment
Overworking	Maintaining a reasonable work load	Leave your work at the office—and leave the office on time
Taking a loved one for granted	Regularly affirming that person's value	Do at least one thing each day to make that person feel cherished
Intending to exercise but never getting around to it	Making physical health a priority	Exercise twenty minutes each morning
Vegging in front of the television to avoid tackling the task at hand	Living life fully and making the most of limited time	Turn off the television for an entire week
Not making time for God	Nurturing a strong spiritual life	Pray, meditate, or read your Bible for fifteen minutes each day
Not spending quality time with your family	Staying closely connected to loved ones	Sit down with your family for at least one meal each day

Once you've evaluated the change for seven days, commit to it for two more weeks. Twenty-one days is the amount of time, on average, that it takes to make, change, or form a habit. If you can do something for three weeks, you can keep going indefinitely.

Keep in mind that while small but significant changes can help you break some of your unhealthy patterns, other areas of your life may need massive change. Incorporating this small seven-day change is just an exercise in how to build momentum. Consider it a "warmup," so to speak, as you condition yourself and develop the strength to take even bigger strides forward.

The key to a transformed life is to start making changes *now*. Begin today to replace your self-sabotaging habits with healthy alternatives.

Closing the Gap

Focus Your Thoughts

If you're feeling overwhelmed by the thought of how many changes you need to make, meditate on the truth that only by embracing change can you achieve God's vision for your life: "Let us lay aside every weight, and the sin which so easily ensnares us, and let us run with endurance the race that is set before us" (Hebrews 12:1).

Use Your Words Wisely

Divide a sheet of paper into three columns. In the first column list your habitually negative thoughts, attitudes, and actions. In the second column identify the good habits you would like to see replace your old patterns. In the third column note one action you can take to incorporate the positive responses in your daily life.

Target Your Actions

Choose one small, meaningful change to incorporate into your life for the next seven days. Once that change is ingrained in your response pattern, challenge yourself to another seven-day change. Continue building momentum to close the gaps in your life.

Energize Your Spirit

God, help me identify the self-defeating patterns in my life and exercise the discipline to make meaningful changes that will help transform me into the person You designed me to be. Amen.

Seventeen

Are You Speaking Death into Your Life?

Eliminate Negative Talk from Your Daily Conversation

When I was burdened by credit-card debt, I constantly thought about and verbalized what a burden that debt was in my life. I frequently declared that I didn't know how I'd ever dig my way out of the hole I was in. My situation felt overwhelming at the time, and I reinforced my sense of desperation with my words. When I created a financial vision—clearly identifying where I stood and laying out a strategy for resolving my problems—my words changed. When my words changed, my hope was rekindled, and I moved to action. My focus moved to all of the exciting opportunities and financial peace my recovery would bring—and the situation turned around.

I've learned through that experience and others that we cannot close the gaps in our lives by focusing on them. We must look past the gap to the other side and express our goals verbally. Why? Because by centering our words on the positive, we begin directing our thoughts rather than allowing our thoughts to direct us.

"Death and life are in the power of the tongue," Proverbs 18:21 tells us. Unless you truly understand and act on the wisdom of this scripture, you will be continually held back by the damning words of your own mouth. You can literally "speak death" into your life by not paying attention to how you speak.

Your words both create and reinforce thoughts in your mind, whether for good or bad. A person who says, "I could never do that," likely won't. One who insists, "Oh, I am much too afraid to move forward in that area of my life," will likely remain right where she is.

We so regularly hear and speak negative words that we can begin to think it's normal. The truth is that negative talk is against God's will, yet it is a natural tendency of human nature that we must consistently resist. "No man can tame the tongue," James 3:8 warns. "It is a restless evil, full of deadly poison" (NIV). That scripture reveals the potential danger of our words and acknowledges the struggle we all endure to control them.

The words you use are a powerful force in dictating the action you will take. That is why I've provided an exercise at the end of each chapter for "using your words wisely" before I suggest a specific action to take. If you maintain an awareness of the words that come out of your mouth and ensure that they are empowering and uplifting, you will change your life. Consider this verse from James 3:3-6:

> When we put bits into the mouths of horses to make them obey us, we can turn the whole animal. Or take ships as an example. Although they are so large and are driven by strong winds, they are steered by a very small rudder wherever the pilot wants to go.

Likewise the tongue is a small part of the body, but it makes great boasts. Consider what a great forest is set on fire by a small spark. The tongue also is a fire, a world of evil among the parts of the body. It corrupts the whole person, sets the whole course of his life on fire, and is itself set on fire by hell. (NIV)

The negative words you speak can destroy relationships, self-confidence, hope, and progress. You can talk yourself out of your own destiny by the words you allow to come out of your mouth! You can convince others that you aren't worth their time just by talking down about yourself or using words that turn them away. Conversely, by choosing to salt your conversation with uplifting words and positive perspectives, you can pave the way to success in your relationships, career, and other areas of life.

I encourage you to make an effort to be particularly aware of how you talk about yourself, your life, and your dreams. You may be amazed by how often negative talk appears in your conversations. Following are some examples of the type of negative comments you might hear from yourself or others.

1. Negative reinforcement. This includes comments that underscore your weaknesses or fears.

- "I'm too afraid to do that."
- "I hate my thighs/hair/feet/skin/lips/legs/any part of my body!"
- "I don't have enough experience."
- "I'm ill. Who knows if I'll ever get better?"
- "I can't do that."
- "I'm not good enough/smart enough/attractive enough."

These words need to be replaced by remarks that uplift you and point you toward God's thoughts of you.

2. Claims of powerlessness. This type of speech puts the responsibility for your emotions in another person's hands.

- "She made me do it."
- "You make me feel stupid."
- "He doesn't make me happy anymore."
- "She made me so angry, I couldn't help myself."

As we've seen before, regardless of what another person does, you choose your reaction, and therefore you are responsible for your own feelings and actions in every circumstance.

3. Negative absolutes. This includes broad, negative generalizations based upon limited information, negative experiences, and even stereotypes.

- "Everybody is against me."
- "My life is always a struggle."
- "I'll never get out of debt."
- "I'll always _____."
- "All the good men are taken."
- "My relationships never last."
- "I never have any money. It's not fair."
- "No one appreciates me."
- "All women are after my money."

These kinds of comments limit your options and thinking and need to be countered by honesty and open-mindedness.

4. Wishful speaking. I urge you to eliminate two words in particular from your vocabulary: "wish" and "should."

- "I wish I could have that."
- "I should not have made that error."
- "I should be further along in my life by now."
- "I wish I didn't have to deal with this anymore."

Should is a word filled with regret, obligation, second-guessing, even guilt. *Wish* is disempowering; it indicates that you have no control over the outcome of this circumstance.

To break free from each of these four types of negative comments, you'll have to move beyond reporting disappointing circumstances to forecasting a positive future outcome. Here are some examples of what I mean:

- "I don't have the money I would like at this point, but God is meeting my needs, and I look forward to achieving financial stability."

- "I may be sick right now, but this situation is temporary. I hope to be feeling healthy again soon."

- "Some of my past relationships ended badly, but I am learning from them so that I can turn things around. I trust God to help me be my best and enjoy healthy, lasting relationships."

The idea is not to pretend that your situation is perfect; instead, the goal is to avoid dwelling verbally on your disappointments. This principle is based on Proverbs 26:20: "Without wood a fire goes out; without gossip a quarrel dies down" (NIV). When you stop "gossiping" about yourself and your problems, they'll seem to grow smaller and consume less of your energy. By speaking edifying words or by simply being silent on a matter, you steer your thoughts away from the problem and toward the solution. "Pleasant words are a honeycomb, sweet to the soul and healing to the bones" (Proverbs 16:24, NIV).

Even the smallest phrases and words can affect how you see the world and your possibilities. As a child, you probably heard adults say, "If you can't say anything good, don't say anything at all." This principle is important to remember, especially when you are talking about yourself and your circumstances. Words can reinforce your thoughts and, therefore, direct your actions. That's why it is possible to combat negative thought patterns and unhealthy behavioral cycles by changing how you talk. When you hear yourself saying things that are not true or are negative and self-sabotaging, stop yourself. Be quiet for a moment; then change your words to something constructive and empowering and true.

For example, when you're tempted to declare, "She made me do it," instead tell the truth: "I allowed her to influence me to do something I regret." This places the responsibility for your actions fully on your shoulders, which in itself is empowering. Instead of complaining, "I wish I didn't have to deal with this anymore," say, "I don't want to deal with this anymore. What are my options to change the situation?"

You gain strength when you speak only words of truth and power. By "truth" I do not simply mean *your* truth. That would be of no benefit because you could choose to repeat only the negative truths about yourself, reminding yourself constantly of your mistakes, failures, fears, and regrets. Many people speak only the negative truth about themselves, allowing their past failures and mistakes to hold them back.

When I encourage you to speak only words of truth, I am asking you to seek first what God thinks about your circumstances, issues, and challenges—and allow only God's truth to come out of your mouth. When the Enemy repeats to you time and again, "Who do you think you are? You can't do that. You're not good enough," you *must* fight back with, "I am a child of God." "I can do all things through Christ who strengthens me" (Philippians 4:13). "If God is for [me], who can be against [me]?" (Romans 8:31)

Sometimes you may not feel as if God's truth is real in your life, but you cannot be victorious by speaking what you feel. You must speak what you know to be true based on God's Word and His promises. By repeating aloud truthful words that you may have trouble believing or feeling, you can influence your thought patterns, transform your attitude, and direct yourself toward actions that will move you closer to where you want to be.

Closing the Gap

Focus Your Thoughts

Meditate on the following scripture, and allow its truth to guide your conversation today: "When we put bits into the mouths of horses to make them obey us, we can turn the whole animal. Or take ships as an example. Although they are so large and are driven by strong winds, they are steered by a very small rudder wherever the pilot wants to go. Likewise the tongue is a small part of the body, but it makes great boasts. Consider what a great forest is set on fire by a small spark" (James 3:3-5, NIV).

Use Your Words Wisely

Pinpoint a specific area in which you have been stuck in a rut of negativity. Recall the negative words you have used in referring to the situation or person. Think of neutral or positive words to describe the situation, then add to those some powerful words to describe your vision for the situation once it's resolved.

Target Your Actions

Strive today to take note of every word you speak. Be aware of the impact of your words on your frame of mind. Remember, words hold the power of death and life, so choose them carefully.

Energize Your Spirit

Lord, please free me from negative words and negative attitudes. I don't want to pretend life is perfect, but I also don't want to be pessimistic. When negative words come to mind, make me instantly aware of them and empower me to resist the temptation to speak them. Help me speak in ways that are empowering, wise, and uplifting. Keep me mindful of Your truth when doubts and fears crop up. Amen.

Eighteen

Do You Talk Too Much?

Practice the Art of Keeping Quiet

Every time I encounter Jean, a business colleague, she is planning to start a new business, write a book, or implement a new idea. Animated with excitement, she will go into great detail about her plans and ideas.

Early on in our relationship, I made a point of listening and trying to help her brainstorm ways to turn her vision into reality. Over time, however, it became apparent that Jean is all talk. And in the few instances where she has moved forward on an idea, she hasn't carried it out with excellence.

I continue to like her as a person, but I don't indulge in long conversations about her plans and ideas because I don't take them seriously. I don't feel that she is intentionally lying to me, but I do think she talks too

---

Portions of this chapter are adapted from the author's radio program, *The Good Life*, ABC Radio, May 2003.

much. What I mean is, the words she speaks don't match her actions or the outcomes she predicts. Over time I've noticed that others appear to have similar feelings about her capabilities. Jean, despite all her positive qualities and persuasive communication skills, has hurt herself by her incessant talking. She has lost credibility with those who might be able to help in her endeavors. If she invested less energy in her words and more in her actions and listening skills, I believe she would find success more quickly and easily, primarily because others would be much more interested in supporting her along the way.

Relationships play a crucial role in helping us move to the next level, but those relationships must be based on trust. Trust, of course, goes both ways: You trust others to help you realize your destiny. They trust you to do what you say you'll do and to behave consistently with your words. I call this *verbal integrity*. People with verbal integrity have earned a reputation for being trustworthy. They not only make a practice of following through on promises and commitments, but they guard their conversation against overcommitment and exaggeration of their abilities or intentions.

Is your tendency to talk too much undermining your verbal integrity? The following are just a few indicators to watch out for in your behavior:

- Saying things about people that you would never say in their presence
- Making a promise to yourself and breaking it
- Making a promise to someone else and breaking it
- Telling "fibs"
- Exaggerating
- Arriving late for a scheduled appointment
- Saying you will do something and not following through

- Doing anything that doesn't line up with what you say
- Speaking in a way that is not aligned with your values or beliefs
- Being too outspoken.
- Complaining about problems but never taking constructive steps to resolve them.

If you've established a habit of talking too much, or if you fear you've damaged your integrity with your words—most of us have been guilty of this at some time—let the following rules guide your future conversations:

1. Speak through your actions. Rather than talking about what you are going to do, just do it!

2. Choose to be content with who you are and what you have, no matter the circumstances. You don't need to impress anyone else.

3. If you cannot keep your word, say so. When you are not going to be able to live up to your word, let the other person know as soon as possible. Have respect for the impact your change in plans may have on the other person, and have respect for your word by admitting when you cannot keep it.

4. Resist the temptation to brag, exaggerate, or lie—no matter how small you feel the lie is.

5. Never speak words because they are popular or represent the values of those you want to influence unless those words also represent your own values and beliefs.

6. Stand up for yourself. You can disagree and speak your mind respectfully. Often this requires you to be quiet, observe, and hold your peace, and then to speak at the appropriate time in the appropriate way. You can be a catalyst for change by using your words effectively and at the right time.

7. Focus on solutions rather than complaints. Complaining drains your energy and the energy of those around you. Rather than wasting energy murmuring and complaining, use it to brainstorm solutions that could resolve your complaints altogether.

Perhaps verbal integrity isn't an issue for you, but still you talk too much. Let me explain: As we've seen, the words we use hold many good possibilities for change. They can heal relationships, change attitudes, communicate ideas, and serve as a conduit for peace. But words hold just as many negative possibilities for destruction. In moments they can tear down relationships, self-esteem, and dreams that have been in the making for years.

The book of Proverbs is filled with warnings about the importance of being prudent in our speech:

Even a fool is thought wise if he keeps silent,
  and discerning if he holds his tongue. (Proverbs 17:28, NIV)

The words of a man's mouth are deep waters,
  but the fountain of wisdom is a bubbling brook.
    (Proverbs 18:4, NIV)

A fool's lips bring him strife,
  and his mouth invites a beating.
A fool's mouth is his undoing,
  and his lips are a snare to his soul.
The words of a gossip are like choice morsels;
  they go down to a man's inmost parts. (Proverbs 18:6-8, NIV)

A gossip betrays a confidence;
> so avoid a man who talks too much. (Proverbs 20:19, NIV)

Like a club or a sword or a sharp arrow
> is the man who gives false testimony against his neighbor.
>> (Proverbs 25:18, NIV)

Without wood a fire goes out;
> without gossip a quarrel dies down. (Proverbs 26:20, NIV)

Let another praise you, and not your own mouth;
> someone else, and not your own lips. (Proverbs 27:2, NIV)

The Bible is filled with many more observations about the power of our words. Yet few of us have taken to heart the importance of these truths. We haven't learned to take control of how and when we speak.

Eva, for example, recognized that she was angry about some issues in her marriage. However, she didn't realize that the problem was not just her temper but what came out of her mouth when her temper flared up. She said she wanted to improve her relationship with her husband of two years, yet she allowed her aggravation with her new stepdaughter to result in yelling matches. Having grown up in a household in which yelling was a way of life, she didn't see how divisive her words and tone of voice were to her relationships. As the rift between Eva and her stepdaughter widened, so did the gap in her marriage. Things continued to decline until she sought counseling and learned to use her words more wisely.

Is it possible that, as with Eva, your words are affecting your ability to succeed at work or in your relationships? Ask yourself the following questions to determine if exercising more self-control in your conversations may be the key to closing a gap in your life:

1. Do I often find myself wishing I could take back something I've said or written? The blessing and curse of words is the same: They cannot be easily undone. Once you fire off that scathing e-mail, it's a permanent record. Once those unkind words leave your lips, they're imprinted indelibly on someone's memory. That's why it's critical to choose your words carefully. Whether you're communicating with your children or dealing with a conflict in your work environment, you can tear down a relationship or build it up within a matter of seconds. Make sure your words do the latter.

2. When I hear gossip, do I give in to the urge to participate, or do I change the flow of the conversation to something more positive? I know, I know. Gossip is terribly tempting, especially given the politics so often at play in the workplace. But I encourage you to make a decision to steer clear of it. When you embrace all that is possible for your life, you'll become much less concerned with negative conversation. Be vigilant about any negative words you allow into your environment. Just being present in the midst of such talk can rope you into awkward situations or unfairly influence your attitude and words so that you begin responding more negatively than usual.

3. Do I react to others verbally while I am angry or frustrated, or do I take time to calm down before speaking about an emotionally charged topic? Nine times out of ten, waiting before you respond to a situation that has you emotionally keyed up will result in a much calmer and wiser response. Depending on the level of your anger or frustration, it's prudent to wait a set period of time (it could be ten minutes, twenty-four hours, or more) before approaching someone about a sensitive issue. Otherwise you may phrase your response too harshly or say something you will later regret. Your communication will be clearer and more effective when you have time to take the emotion out of your response and think about the words you want to use.

4. When I am feeling down about my circumstances, do I murmur or complain? Life certainly can be frustrating at times, and you may even have a legitimate reason to be upset, but don't get caught up in a habit of complaining. It drains your energy and the energy of those around you. Murmuring and complaining sap your strength and take the focus off God and His power to change the situation or teach you needed lessons. Resisting the urge to complain doesn't mean that you can't stand up for yourself when you've been mistreated. It doesn't mean that you won't confront problems in a proactive way. Quite the opposite, actually. It means that if you aren't going to work toward a solution, then you'll be quiet about the problem. If, however, you have an idea for improving the situation, you'll present it in a positive, forthright manner.

5. Do I tend to dominate conversations, always feeling the need to voice my opinion or win an argument? Some of the wisest people in the world speak the least. They are secure in who they are and don't feel the need to prove their worthiness by expressing their opinions and knowledge at every opportunity. Instead, they listen without judgment. Through their listening they learn and gain wisdom. Practice being quiet, even when you feel the urge to let everyone hear your opinion. Of course, there are times when expressing your opinion is critical. Learn to discern the difference between speaking out of insecurity or a need for attention and speaking out of authenticity and for mutual benefit.

6. Do I brag frequently about past achievements? You can alienate others by overplaying your past achievements. Certainly your prior victories build a foundation on which to move forward and experience greater levels of success, but talking too much about them is not a constructive use of those achievements. Often it indicates an overemphasis on what you've done as opposed to who you are. Past performance is not necessarily an indicator of future success—whether your past is something you love to talk about or something you'd rather not discuss. Question your motives when you are tempted to bring up your past achievements. Before you begin talking about them, ask yourself, "Is what I want to say necessary? Will it benefit this conversation, the other person, or God's ability to work through me?" If the answers are yes, proceed. If the answers are no, then no matter how much you are itching to brag, keep your words to yourself. As Proverbs 27:2 advises, "Let another praise you, and not your own mouth; someone else, and not your own lips" (NIV).

7. Do I offer too much detail about myself, my desires, and my plans to people who may not have my best interests at heart? Another reason it is important not to talk too much is that not everyone is interested in seeing you succeed, even when they act or speak as if they do. You may avoid the pain of betrayal by being cautious about sharing the most intimate details of your dreams and goals.

In the Sermon on the Mount, Jesus promised, "Blessed are the meek, for they shall inherit the earth" (Matthew 5:5). Meekness can be defined as "strength under control." In other words, you do not have to impress others and display outward signs of strength in order to be powerful or prove your potential. At times it can feel nearly impossible to hold your tongue, but some of the most successful people in the world have learned to be quiet in situations in which others may have used their platform to talk too much.

Legendary musician Miles Davis set trends in music for four decades, making a mark that will impact jazz for years to come. Certainly, he had a platform from which to talk and draw attention to himself, but that was not his focus. He appeared to be concerned not about attracting the spotlight but about honing his craft, creating meaningful music, and entertaining others. He was known to be a man of very few words. He rarely gave interviews and sometimes did not even talk during his concerts. He centered his energies on his passion, purpose, and gift of music—and achieved amazing success.

Such reserve seems rare in a culture obsessed with sharing far too much information, be it on tell-all talk shows or in celebrity-obsessed magazines. One indicator of our society's tendency to talk too much is the news media. In recent years many journalists and networks have adopted a style of defining the meaning of events for viewers, readers, and listeners rather than reporting facts and allowing audiences to draw their own conclusions. Brian Lamb, founder of C-SPAN, is a great example of someone who subscribes to the philosophy of not talking too much. When you want to watch and listen to the political process unfiltered by opinionated predictions, assessments, and commentary, C-SPAN offers a refreshing alternative. Early critics of the network didn't believe it would attract viewers, but its popularity can be explained in large part by the fact that many people appreciate an unfiltered look at the political process in action, and many others appreciate an opportunity to share their opinions without fear of attack. Hosts of the daily shows on C-SPAN field calls from viewers with a variety of opinions—sometimes very extreme opinions—but the hosts do not give commentary or counterpoints or argue with callers. Instead, they ask questions such as "What makes you say that?" or "Why do you feel that way?"

You, too, may find these questions helpful as you seek to listen more than you speak. By phrasing your responses this way, you demonstrate respect for the other person's insights and opinions rather than calling attention to your own. As you practice the art of keeping quiet, you will begin to see improvements in your relationships and in your attitude about your circumstances. And you'll find that you're becoming more of the person God intends you to be.

Closing the Gap

Focus Your Thoughts
Memorize and meditate on this scripture: "Let every man be swift to hear, slow to speak, slow to wrath" (James 1:19).

Use Your Words Wisely
Decide not to share every idea that comes to you. Seek out a coach, advisor, or friend with whom you can brainstorm and plan, but refrain from talking about your plans with too many people until they have come to fruition. Not everyone needs to know everything that goes on in your life or every idea or plan you are considering.

Target Your Actions
Practice remaining quiet even when you feel like proving a point, sounding smart, or attracting attention. Notice what happens when you speak less.

Energize Your Spirit
Lord, please help me discern when to talk and when to keep quiet. Give me the wisdom and the desire to listen to others without interrupting, to engage in conversation without dominating, and to have integrity in all that I say. Amen.

Nineteen

Have You Skipped a Step?

Lay the Groundwork for Success

Marian felt stuck in her career. On the verge of completing her internship requirements to become a licensed therapist, she felt sure she wanted to open a private coaching practice and also pursue doctoral studies. At the same time, as a fairly new bride who was adjusting to life as a wife and stepmother, she said she wanted to keep family life as a top priority.

A quick look at her daily schedule indicated that her actions were in conflict with her stated priority. Her heavy schedule of commitments was creating intense pressure and stress for her and her entire family. Adding even more to her burden was Marian's self-imposed goal of finishing her doctorate by the age of thirty.

When she came to me for coaching to help get her private practice off the ground, I asked, "What's your biggest priority right now?"

"My family," she said, then hesitated. "But I haven't been acting like it. I haven't wanted to give up my goals and my things."

"Have you given yourself the space to give attention to your new marriage and stepchildren?" I asked.

She sat for a moment, then replied with a guilty tinge in her voice. "No, I really haven't," she revealed. Her schedule had been rather jam-packed even before she married, and now there was absolutely no margin.

"Would you consider a variation of your business goal?" I asked. "What if you drop the coaching aspect for now and just focus on gaining more experience in the areas of counseling you've already trained in?"

She paused for a long while. "I would consider that," she said. Then, after a few more seconds of thought, she added. "Actually, that would take a lot of pressure off me. I guess I don't have to do it right now."

Marian was quite capable and had a successful career ahead of her, but she'd been overwhelmed by the mistaken belief that she needed to pursue all her dreams at the same time. As we talked she decided to postpone her coaching goal for a year and a half, wait to pursue her doctorate until she had gained more practical experience, and focus more energy on strengthening her marriage and family. As we continued coaching, I watched the transformation as she released everything that held her back from the goal she claimed as her priority: a peaceful, joyful family life.

By focusing on her marriage, Marian was not only doing the will of God, which calls wives to make their husbands their top priority behind their relationship with God; she was also building a stronger relationship with her family, an investment that will decrease stress and provide a secure foundation for pursuing a business in the future. Getting her own personal life in order will help Marian later succeed as a therapist and coach.

Like Marian, many of us get so excited by our vision that we stumble over ourselves, trying to meet all our goals at once. The reality is that we need to approach our vision in an orderly fashion, taking deliberate steps to lay the groundwork for our future goals.

Proverbs 24:27 says, "Finish your outdoor work and get your fields ready; after that, build your house" (NIV). The *Life Application Study Bible* interprets that verse like this: "If a farmer builds his house in the spring, he will miss the planting season and go a year without food. If a businessman invests his money in a house while his business is struggling to grow, he may lose both. It is possible to work hard and still lose everything if the timing is wrong or the resources to carry it out are not in place."

When you've laid out a clear and compelling vision, it's normal to get so excited that you're tempted to skip ahead and force things to happen before their natural timing. But God is a God of order. Consider the seven days of Creation. God didn't create animals until after He created the plants and other resources to sustain them.

Laying the proper groundwork for success means creating the space to tend to your priorities and giving yourself the time to prepare for long-term goals. Not everything you want in life has to happen right now. Bringing your vision to fruition is a process.

I recently received an e-mail from a reader who was distressed about launching her business. Her message revealed that she was essentially homeless, sleeping at friends' houses for a few days at a time, and unable to pay her bills or take care of her most basic needs. Despite the fact that she had no money to support herself, she was so determined to focus on her business that she didn't want to work even a part-time job. It simply had not occurred to her that she needed to "get her fields ready." I encouraged her to realize that her first priority had to be laying the basic foundation of her life—a place to live and a sustainable income to cover her expenses—before she attempted to build the framework of her vision.

The vision is enticing, exciting. And laying groundwork is often unpleasant, unglamorous, and thankless work. It can require you to make changes that make you uncomfortable or to deal with issues you'd rather avoid. You may be tempted to skip ahead to those aspects of building your vision that bring you joy, but if you do, you'll miss essential steps that can lead you to the level of success God desires for you. You may watch helplessly as your dreams come tumbling down without the proper support structures.

If, however, you commit to completing first steps first and approaching your goals in an orderly fashion, your vision will stand firm even when the storms of life crash against it, because you have laid the proper foundation.

Closing the Gap

Focus Your Thoughts

Consider your vision. What do you find most compelling about it? Why does it move you to excitement? What aspects of pursuing your vision do you find troubling?

Use Your Words Wisely

Identify, in writing, the steps you must take in order to lay the strongest foundation for your vision. Give special consideration to the aspects you previously identified as troubling, to be sure you're not skipping over anything.

Target Your Actions

Today, decide what foundational elements you must focus on to increase your chances for success. Take action toward completing one of those fundamental steps.

Energize Your Spirit

God, give me the patience and discipline to take the steps I need to take in order to lay a firm foundation. Show me how to build the life You've designed for me. Amen.

Twenty

Are You Always Running Behind?

Regain Control of Your Schedule

Vickie was a successful business owner admired by her clients and sincere in her desire to serve others. But a seemingly endless string of emergencies was diverting her energy and attention from the tasks she deemed priorities. Even as she saw crises heading straight for her door, she was too busy dealing with the crisis at hand to avoid the next predicament. Her mode of operation, which led to one financial surprise after another, irritated Vickie's husband and created a constant source of stress for her. Her daily planner was filled with looming deadlines—looming *extended* deadlines, in fact, because she was rarely able to complete any project on time.

Since her teen years she'd always operated best on an adrenaline rush, but now Vickie was at a crossroads. Chronic stress-related headaches had

---

Portions of this chapter are adapted from the author's radio program, *The Good Life*, ABC Radio, May 2003.

plagued her for more than a decade, and Vickie was ready for a change. If she was to succeed at the next level, it would take more than adrenaline to fuel her success—particularly if she wanted to maintain her health in the process.

"Do you see how your mode of operation is hurting you?" I asked.

"Kind of," she replied hesitantly, not fully understanding how her behavior was affecting her stress level and limiting her success.

"You've indicated that you are behind on your taxes, your annual health exam, a major project, and two proposals, not to mention the fact that several things need to be fixed on your car," I said. "And you have another whole list of viable and important goals you consider priorities yet are unable to attend to. How does it make you feel thinking about all those things on your plate?"

"Wow. I hadn't thought of them all in the same context," she replied. "I'm exhausted and overwhelmed. I feel like I'm failing, but I guess I really don't have the time to get it all done."

"What if the issue isn't really a lack of time?" I probed. "I mean, you've said before that this is how you've always operated."

"Well, if it isn't time, what is it?" she asked, perplexed.

It wasn't one single issue that held Vickie back from gaining control of her schedule, but several. First, as we discussed in chapter 16, she had conditioned herself to respond to time issues with some rather unhealthy habits. Her expectations of what she could accomplish in a given amount of time were unrealistic. She would create a to-do list packed with fifteen hours' worth of activities and insist they could be accomplished in eight or nine hours.

Second, she had too many goals to successfully manage at once and was afraid to let any of them go for fear that she would let the wrong goal fall by the wayside. All her goals may have been good ones—and quite possibly all will be accomplished eventually. They just couldn't all be accomplished at once.

Third, Vickie allowed fear to control her schedule rather than listening for the voice of God and those nudges in her spirit that were trying to lead her in a particular direction. As a result, Vickie became overwhelmed, frustrated, and not nearly as effective as she could have been.

With so many projects, priorities, and goals, she had difficulty concentrating on one thing at a time and was regularly distracted. If the goal of the moment was spending time with her husband, she was distracted by a work-related phone call. If the goal was going to an overdue doctor's appointment, she might become distracted by emergency car trouble and never make her appointment. Then the appointment would go unscheduled for two more months. She had created a schedule that seemed out of control, but there was hope for change if she confronted the root issues and made the difficult choices to regain control of her life.

Does Vickie's story sound all too familiar? Do you feel as if you are constantly running to catch up? Are you frequently late for appointments and deadlines? Do you simply run out of time before getting to your priorities? Do you neglect—or just forget—to make appointments for preventive maintenance on your house or car or for regular health checkups?

Operating continuously at warp speed is detrimental to your physical, emotional, and spiritual energy levels. Even if you feel invigorated by the constantly frantic pace, the stress will eventually catch up with you. In fact, you may find yourself completely exasperated and ready to give up at times. On the few occasions that you manage to meet a deadline, your efforts may be rushed and haphazard.

When you're constantly running behind, it's like not being in position at the starting block when the race official fires the starting gun. Instead of racing to close the gap between you and the finish line, you're just trying to get in position to start. Even if you somehow manage to cross the finish line, it's unlikely that you'll do so in a timely fashion or that you'll feel proud about how you ran the race.

This mode of operation will not help you reach the next level in your life. You are destined for excellence, and that includes excellence in how you operate on a daily basis—giving yourself the time and preparation you need to succeed gracefully.

For the sake of your health and the sanity of those around you, I invite you to regain control of your schedule—and your life. Take an honest look at how you have organized your time, then rearrange things as necessary so that any mistakes, delays, and other surprises won't throw you seriously off course.

Let me illustrate this another way. Just as you have a set amount of income, you have only a limited amount of time, and you need to budget it wisely. You know, for example, that if your financial budget doesn't allow for unexpected expenses, you'll probably end up charging the costs of a needed car repair to your credit card—without a plan in place for paying it off. With each subsequent financial "emergency," you'll dig yourself a little deeper into debt.

The same thing can happen with your time. If you don't budget wisely, creating cushions of time between commitments, an unexpected delay of any kind can create a domino effect in your overly full schedule. With each new interruption or crisis, you'll fall further and further behind.

People who are constantly striving to catch up are hardly in a position to close the gap between where they are and where they want to be. They're barely hanging on to where they are.

The cure for being chronically behind is to acknowledge the problem and then schedule some time to simply catch up. This means saying no to anything new until you have the opportunity to tie up all your loose ends. It may be as simple as setting aside an afternoon to get caught up. Or you may need to schedule time each day or each week for several months just to resolve your backlog of commitments and projects.

After you've taken the time you need to get caught up, it is critical that you not return to the same behaviors that landed you in trouble in the first place. Develop the systems you need to stay organized and to plan ahead. Here are a few guidelines to get you started:

1. *Be willing to make serious changes.* Vickie made a major change by cutting back her work dramatically until she could get a handle on her schedule. It was extremely uncomfortable at first but ultimately resulted in a more relaxed and healthy outlook, less stress, and more joy in her life.

2. *Identify your true priorities.* If you want to live an authentic life, you must get in touch with what really matters to you and align your actions with those goals.

3. *Notice how you spend your time.* For one week keep a notepad with you and record how you spend your time. Be honest, especially when you find yourself wasting time. This is an exercise in discovering how you spend your time, not beating yourself up for wasting it!

4. *Drop or modify activities that are not top priorities.* You have only so many hours in each day. Make sure you invest your energy in doing the things that really matter rather than allowing your time to be consumed with activities that no longer serve your purposes.

5. *Plan your schedule six to twelve months in advance.* Obviously, you won't know the day-to-day detail of most of your schedule this far out, but you can predict periods of time when you will need to allot more time for certain priorities. This will allow you to plan important events, such as vacations, and rearrange your schedule to accommodate them.

6. *Learn to anticipate potential bumps in the road and resolve them before they become major obstacles.* Proverbs 22:3 says, "A prudent man sees danger and takes refuge, but the simple keep going and suffer for it" (NIV). You must become realistic about the amount of time and energy you need to meet your essential obligations and priorities. By realistically gauging your necessary investment, you can better schedule your life, plan ahead, and stop racing to get to the starting line.

At first glance, these principles may seem like simple time management, but in reality they offer you something more: freedom. When you have the time to plan and the breathing room to experiment, you free yourself to take advantage of opportunities that others are too consumed to even notice. Regaining control of your schedule will help you find the time and energy to close the gaps in your life.

Closing the Gap

Focus Your Thoughts
Take some time to contemplate what you would gain from being in control of your time and having a reasonable schedule. Envision how your life could be different in this regard.

Use Your Words Wisely

Practice saying no to new tasks, goals, and projects until you gain control over or let go of the ones to which you are currently committed.

Target Your Actions

In what areas of your life are you running behind? How much time do you need to catch up? Commit to scheduling a block of time each week to catch up—for as long as it takes—and write it in your appointment calendar. If you're not running behind, ask yourself what it would take to be ahead of schedule in the key areas of your life, then set aside time to build that cushion into your life.

Energize Your Spirit

God, I am tired of rushing through life. Help me get organized, meet my commitments, and not become overwhelmed by my many responsibilities. Grant me the wisdom to discern between important priorities and distractions that threaten to clutter my schedule and that take me away from the things You want me to accomplish. Amen.

Twenty-One

What's Distracting You?

Focus on Your Priorities

Whether your goal is to strengthen your marriage, build up your retirement account, or conquer a looming deadline, you've probably noticed how frequently distractions creep into your life and prevent you from being as productive as you'd like.

Unnecessary e-mails, unexpected phone calls, unplanned purchases, and unscheduled events—not to mention those irresistible brownies in the employee break room—all conspire to divert us from the things we claim are priorities. Even more troublesome are the many activities that sidetrack us from making progress on our path to extraordinary success. Few of us could be accused of idleness, but we're just not busy doing the things that matter most.

Portions of this chapter are adapted from Valorie Burton, The Life Enrichment Challenge, Challenge 1: "I Have a Vision for My Life That Excites and Challenges Me," January 26, 2004, www.BlackAmericaWeb.com.

We can easily spend our entire lives being productive in ways that do not move us any closer to our vision. We can become so caught up in the distractions of life that we completely lose sight of where we were headed. Let me encourage you to begin to view your distractions as the enemy. Deliberate action is vital if you want to prevent that enemy from taking your goals and vision hostage.

The first step in overcoming distractions is to align your daily actions with a very clear set of priorities. Make a list of your top priority in each of the five key areas of your life—your relationships, career, finances and resources, physical health and environments, and spiritual life. On a weekly basis, review your calendar and activities to be sure they reflect what you have identified as most important. Your goals and your vision will only become reality if you spend your time doing the types of things that will bring them to life. If you want a better marriage, you'll need to clear room in your schedule for quality time with your spouse. If your goal is to save money for a down payment on your dream home, that may involve cutting back on the weekly trips to the mall. Establish your true priorities, then schedule your days to align with them.

A word of caution regarding to-do lists. While written lists are an important tool for establishing priorities, it is also important to keep your expectations under control. Sometimes a to-do list can get so out of hand that it becomes a distraction. Overwhelmed by the sheer volume of things you want to accomplish, you become unclear about what is a true priority. Limit the number of things you try to do in a day, and always align your to-dos with your priorities. Choose one to three must-do action items for any given day, and consider any other accomplishments a bonus.

Depending on the kinds of gaps you're trying to close in your life, you may find that the only times you have to work on your vision are those moments between work or family responsibilities. Nonetheless, be sure to create focus time. Block out time *every day* to concentrate on your vision. Even if you can only squeeze in fifteen minutes early in the morning, make sure to set aside time in your day with the sole objective of taking the next step toward achieving your goal. The action for the day could be as simple as a three-minute phone call, but if you don't block out time to do it, you could find yourself postponing your next move indefinitely—as your vision fades into the distance.

The second step in conquering your distractions is to identify the biggest culprits. To fight effectively, you must know who your enemy is. Is it the telephone or the television? Clutter covering your kitchen table or unfinished business clogging your desk? Chatty co-workers who want to talk when you want to work? The convenience of the drive-through window when you could save money—and calories—by cooking a meal at home?

Once you have identified the distractions to which you're most vulnerable, ask yourself, "How can I eliminate this distraction?" Create rules that give you the freedom to focus on your priorities. That may mean turning off the new-message alert on your computer or letting phone calls go into voice mail at certain times of the day. Maybe you need to set aside a specific morning each week to clear away your clutter or unfinished business. Do you need to practice saying, "Now's not a good time. Can I catch up with you later?" when a talkative co-worker stops by? Can you drive a different route home so you aren't tempted by the drive-through menu? Remember that while you can't avoid temptation entirely, you can choose to resist it and even take action to minimize it. You are in control of your choices.

Other people's agendas and requests serve as the biggest sources of distractions for most of us. Although some requests are clearly important activities in which you'll want or need to be involved, others simply pull you away from more important opportunities. Rather than allowing yourself to be drawn into an unnecessary commitment of your time and energy, be willing to say no to offers that do not serve a purpose for you or that take too much time away from your priorities. Just because someone asks you to do something does not obligate you to do it. Practice graciously saying no.

Your time is valuable, and gaining control of it is a critical aspect of moving closer to where you want to be in life.

Closing the Gap

Focus Your Thoughts
During the next seven days, notice how you spend your time. Become aware of how often you are diverted from your priorities, and identify what is causing each distraction.

Use Your Words Wisely
Each day for the next seven days, say no to at least one activity or request that doesn't align with your priorities. Once you get comfortable with saying no graciously, you may want to use that skill more often!

Target Your Actions
Identify the activity or time commitment that most obviously distracts you from accomplishing your goals. Reorganize your schedule to fill that space with something more reflective of your priorities.

Energize Your Spirit

God, help me resist the distractions that threaten to throw me off course. Your Word urges me to be wise and make the most of every opportunity [Ephesians 5:15-16]. Give me the wisdom to discern between those activities that simply consume my time and those that further Your purposes. Amen.

Twenty-Two

Do You Give Too Much Weight to the Words of Others?

Discern Where to Turn for Direction

Kay found herself dreading the start of her second year of graduate school. A couple of friends who had graduated from college with her had already settled into jobs where they were making "decent" money. They cautioned her that she was wasting her time and assured her that another nine months of graduate school wouldn't really be of help when she entered the "real world." Frustrated about scraping by on wages from a part-time job and anxious to put her skills to work, Kay couldn't stop thinking about their comments. She was seriously considering giving up on her plans to finish graduate school.

Kay just needed a reminder that she had made a good decision to begin work on her master's degree in film writing. She also needed someone else's perspective. I was delighted when she came to me with her concerns and I was able to offer some fresh insight.

By the time we connected, she had latched on to the assessment of these friends, and then found examples that supported their opinion and caused her to question her plan. "So many people my age are so much further ahead professionally," she insisted.

I was rather perplexed by her statement, since this ambitious young woman had already graduated with honors from a top college, completed internships with a major network television show and two major movie studios, and written the manuscript for her first book. "I haven't met many twenty-three-year-olds who've done as much as you have," I assured her. "Can you name a few?"

She mentioned a handful of A-list celebrities in the entertainment world. "I've been watching *Driven* on VH1," she admitted, referring to the music network's biography show about successful entertainers.

"We'd all be discouraged if we measured our success against the fame-looks-money-status definition that the media portrays for us through celebrities!" I responded. "You can't compare what you want to do with what you've been watching."

Kay chuckled at the thought process that she now recognized was at the root of her discouragement. Her goal is to be a writer of novels and movies, so we explored a more realistic view of success, how long it might take to attain it, and how determined she was to stick with it.

"If you knew that twelve years from now, if you just keep pushing forward, you're going to get your big break and your first movie will hit the big screen, would you give up now?" I asked.

I could hear the sound of optimism and possibility in her voice. "No, absolutely not," she said. "I'd definitely stick with it."

She had her answer. Kay shifted her perspective, stuck with her original plan, and completed graduate school nine months later with the resolve to persevere despite the opinions that had threatened to convince her she was wasting her time.

From time to time we all doubt our decisions and turn to others for insight and direction. When we're feeling held back in a particular area of life, it can be tempting to assume that we don't have the answers that will move us forward. But we must be careful not to discount our own wisdom and inner vision. Listening to the advice of those who know us is not a bad idea, in and of itself. In fact, many times such advice is crucial to gaining a fresh perspective on our situation. However, sometimes the people in our lives speak with such authority that we believe them without questioning their words. Other times we rely too heavily on the validation of those we respect and belittle the wisdom of our own inner voice.

Your inner voice is your spirit, that part of you that communicates with God. The only validation you truly need is confirmation from the Lord, speaking to you in words that align with His character as revealed in the Bible. It's difficult to hear the still, small voice of the Lord when you're paying too close attention to the louder voices that chime in with their opinions.

Here are a few of the signs that indicate you are placing too much importance on the wrong voices:

- In your spirit, you know what you want to do, but you don't move forward because you fear that others won't approve of your chosen direction.

- You never make an important decision without asking someone, "What do you think?"

- You get multiple opinions regarding what you should do about a matter that does not impact the people you are asking.
- You discuss personal and professional decisions with people you do not trust 100 percent to keep the information confidential.
- You pray and contemplate before making a decision, but if someone else disapproves of that decision, you doubt yourself and don't move forward.

It's dangerous to give more weight to the words and opinions of others than to your own inner voice and the Holy Spirit. If you aren't careful, you may find yourself relying more heavily on people's words than on the Word of God. This is not to say that others may not have valuable insight or advice to lend, but you need to guard against placing people on a pedestal as "gurus" who have answers you somehow cannot access.

Clients often come to me as a coach, seeking answers for their lives. My job is not to point them in a particular direction but to help them explore their options and uncover the answers that work best for them. By asking the right questions, I help them thoughtfully ponder the issues and options, turn over stones they may have missed, and more deliberately draw a conclusion.

As I worked through this process with a client named Lisa, we made an interesting discovery about her motivations for seeking out a coach.

Lisa came to me because she was thoroughly stressed by her job and was on the verge of quitting. She had accepted the position primarily because of the prestige associated with it. In her mind, this particular job was a "really big deal." When some important colleagues had made the necessary connections to get her the job, she had left a company she really believed in and moved to a new city, even turning down another position that better fit with the career track in which she desired to succeed. Now, after a year in the position, she was miserable, but she hesitated to leave because of her respect for those who helped her get the job. She was concerned that quitting "too soon" would negatively affect their opinion of her.

To complete the particular project on which she was assigned, Lisa would need to stay for nearly one more year. During our second session she seemed particularly exasperated by the idea of hanging in that long.

"You have a few options," I reminded her. "You could quit right now, if you are ready to do that. You could wait until the project is completed in another ten months. Or you could apply for reassignment within the company. You said that was a possibility, right?"

"You know what, Valorie?" she said. "I think I want you to tell me what to do. I think I'm looking for someone to give me the answer. That's why I hired you as my coach, but that doesn't sound healthy."

"You're right," I agreed. "I could tell you what to do, but I won't. God has given you everything you need to make a decision, and I don't want to get in the way of that."

We continued our session, and she left with the assignment of weighing—on her own—the pros and cons of her options. Two days later she told me that not only had she made her decision but she also realized she had come to me not because she was ready to be coached but because she didn't trust herself enough to make decisions. She decided to work on herself first, then continue with coaching.

It takes a lot of courage to recognize our weaknesses and work to turn them into strengths. Lisa is on her way to doing just that.

When you feel uncertain—a normal part of mapping out the path that will help you reach your goal—be particularly cautious as you discuss your goals and decisions with people. When you feel in your spirit that it is time to break free from something—perhaps a job that's holding you back, a financial situation, or certain lifestyle habits—give more weight to what you know in your spirit than to what others are telling you.

If you decide to listen to others' words, be sure to keep them in proper perspective. Don't allow their words to become your words or permit their fears to direct your thinking. And remember, negative words are not the only things to beware of. If you are successful or admired by people, they may offer only what they think you want to hear. Those who want to get in your good graces, or who simply hold you in high esteem, may lead you to believe that your abilities are greater than they actually are. Sometimes family members will overstate your talents or abilities because they are naturally biased.

Allow your own wisdom and experience and the guidance of the Holy Spirit to help you discern when to listen to others and when to resolutely follow your own inner voice.

Closing the Gap

Focus Your Thoughts

As you seek direction for your life, remember that true wisdom is in keeping with God's priorities, whether it comes from your inner voice or from those around you. Meditate on the following verse, and allow its truth to guide your decisions: "The wisdom that is from above is first pure, then peaceable, gentle, willing to yield, full of mercy and good fruits, without partiality and without hypocrisy" (James 3:17).

Use Your Words Wisely

In your journal, write out your answers to the following questions: In what areas of my life do I tend to be influenced by the words and opinions of others? How do I allow them to influence me?

Target Your Actions

Based on what you learned from the journaling exercise above, what behavior do you need to change, or what choice do you need to make to be true to yourself and God's Word and plan for your life? Set a deadline by which you will take that step; then meet your deadline!

Energize Your Spirit

Father God, please grant me the confidence to trust You to direct and guide me. Help me to clearly know when I should heed the words of others because they line up with Your vision for my life. Strengthen me to overcome any insecurities that tempt me to seek validation from people rather than from You. Amen.

Twenty-Three

Are You Watching for a Window of Opportunity?

Be Ready to Make Your Move

At age forty-three, Thomas Hamill of Macon, Mississippi, seized a potentially dangerous but lucrative opportunity. You may recall his story from the news. Looking to pay off the debts that remained after selling the family dairy farm and hoping to raise money for the heart surgery his wife needed, Hamill accepted a position as a civilian truck driver for an American contractor in Iraq.

He had taken the job recognizing the risks of working in that hostile environment. In April 2004 that potential danger became a reality when Hamill was kidnapped in an insurgent attack on his convoy. Those responsible for the kidnapping vowed to kill Hamill within twelve hours if their demands were not met. They did not make good on their threat, but his whereabouts were unknown for weeks.

Hamill had been held captive for three weeks when a new window of opportunity presented itself. When he heard what sounded like a military convoy passing by the mud farmhouse in which he was being held, he managed to pry open a door and slip out. The convoy had moved on by the time he emerged. Undaunted and so close to freedom, Hamill ran half a mile to catch up with the American troops.

Having been wounded in the initial attack on his convoy, Hamill could have spent his time wallowing in self-pity, obsessed by concerns about his health and absorbed in his dire circumstances. Instead, he remained alert to his surroundings. He even had managed to escape once before, but returned to his captors after finding himself in the middle of the desert without food or water. Rather than allowing himself to be consumed by fear and panic, Hamill had determined to maintain hope and be ready to make his move at the first opportune moment. The same boldness and determination that led him to Iraq rather than waiting for his financial problems to resolve themselves also led him out of a potentially deadly situation.

How do you respond when life takes a dark turn? Perhaps you're facing a difficult time right now. Do you feel backed into a corner by your circumstances? Maybe your situation seems too dire to permit any hope of escape. Your fate appears to be sealed.

Look closely: Can you see a glimmer of hope shining through the darkness? "We know that all things work together for good to those who love God, to those who are the called according to His purpose" (Romans 8:28).

Remember, our circumstances lie within God's control, and He's interested not in our destruction but in our construction—the construction of our character, that is. We are each being built into the persons we must become in order to fulfill His divine purposes for our lives. When you are willing to persevere through suffering or struggles, hope is produced out of your character. "We also rejoice in our sufferings, because we know that suffering produces perseverance; perseverance, character; and character, hope. And hope does not disappoint us, because God has poured out his love into our hearts by the Holy Spirit, whom he has given us" (Romans 5:3-5, NIV).

True hope enables you to remain alert because you expect a turn-around, recognizing that if God is working all things for good, it would be foolish to waste energy on feeling sorry for yourself. At the appointed time—if you are vigilant as well as patient—hope will be fulfilled in a window of opportunity. However, if you are preoccupied with your problems or are wallowing in self-pity, you will miss out on that moment. As the convoy of opportunity hums past your door, you will be oblivious because you are making too much noise at your pity party.

Are you familiar with the New Testament account of the woman with the issue of blood? Most people probably wouldn't have blamed her for feeling sorry for herself. After all, she had endured twelve years of continuous bleeding with no relief. Not only had she endured physical misery, but because of the religious laws of the day, her condition forced her to be separated from others. Even her family and friends would have refused to touch or hug her for fear of being declared "unclean" themselves. Surely this could be considered a cause for depression and self-pity, yet she chose hope and vigilance.

When Jesus came to town, she was prepared to seize the opportunity. With such a crowd, she didn't expect to meet Him or talk to Him—she just hoped to get near Him, believing that if she could only touch the hem of His garment, she would be healed (see Luke 8:43-44). Can you picture her weaving through the crowd, desperate to get closer to the Savior? Then suddenly she sees her opening and reaches through the mob of people pressing against Him. Her fingers brush the hem of His garment. The result is miraculous.

In what area of your life have you been feeling sorry for yourself? Are you ready to close down the pity party and prepare to make your move? You don't have time to sadly contemplate your negative circumstances. The opportunity to transform those circumstances may be passing by just outside your door!

Closing the Gap

Focus Your Thoughts

When you feel discouraged by your circumstances, meditate on the truth of Romans 8:28: "We know that all things work together for good to those who love God, to those who are the called according to His purpose."

Use Your Words Wisely

Examine your conversation for signs of self-pity. Replace those negative comments with hopeful words that reflect the hope you have for the future.

Target Your Actions

In what area of your life are you watching for a window of opportunity? Clarify how you will recognize it, and identify what action you will take when it comes. What can you do to nurture hope while you're waiting?

Energize Your Spirit

Dear God, I thank You today for giving me a hope and a future! I thank You for every blessing in my life. Despite any adversities or challenges I face, I am grateful to You for sustaining me. Help me to be vigilant in seeking opportunities to close the gap in areas of my life that at times seem hopeless. Grant me the grace and discipline to persevere until my breakthrough comes! Amen.

Twenty-Four

Are You Relying on God?

Maximize Your Spiritual Leverage

You often hear the word *leverage* in business settings. It carries the idea of accomplishing more with the same or fewer resources. Leverage is a crucial factor not only in business but also in personal and spiritual growth. As we'll see in chapter 29, surrounding yourself with a support team provides leverage that can help propel you toward success more quickly and with less effort on your part. Similarly, you will more easily overcome obstacles and defeat your fears when you maximize your spiritual leverage.

Spiritual leverage can perhaps best be described with the scripture, "If God is for us, who can be against us?" (Romans 8:31). When you are connected to God in a strong relationship, He provides the supernatural strength to propel you forward even when you are exhausted and cannot see where you are headed. God will give you power to move forward despite the forces working to hold you back. In fact, without spiritual leverage, you will always wear yourself out trying to accomplish things in your own strength. When you instead place your trust in God and allow Him to direct your paths, He will use you in ways that are beyond all you could ask or imagine (see Ephesians 3:20). Proverbs 21:30 tells us, "There is no wisdom, no insight, no plan that can succeed against the LORD" (NIV).

Throughout the Old Testament, the people of Israel provide a picture of what can happen when spiritual leverage is put to work. As Joshua prepared to lead the Israelites into the Promised Land, God had given him this promise: "As I was with Moses, so I will be with you; I will never leave you nor forsake you.... Have I not commanded you? Be strong and courageous. Do not be terrified; do not be discouraged, for the LORD your God will be with you wherever you go" (Joshua 1:5,9, NIV). Time and again the people of Israel entered into battle against forces that were larger, stronger, and better equipped. But when they were walking in obedience to God, the Israelites achieved victories that could not possibly have been explained in human terms—sometimes without even having to fight.

In the New Testament Jesus reaffirmed the importance of our reliance on God if we are to fulfill His vision for our lives: "I am the vine, you are the branches. He who abides in Me, and I in him, bears much fruit; for without Me you can do nothing" (John 15:5). He not only promised to meet our needs as the bread and water of life, He offered to ease our load along the way: "Come to me, all you who are weary and burdened, and I will give you rest. Take my yoke upon you and learn from me, for I am gentle and humble in heart, and you will find rest for your souls. For my yoke is easy and my burden is light" (Matthew 11:28-30, NIV).

Talk about spiritual leverage! With Jesus you can handle more challenges with less worry. You can have joy in the midst of crisis. Others may wonder at your response to seemingly insurmountable circumstances and thirst after what you have. When that happens, God is able to use your situation to bring others closer to Him.

Spiritual leverage, however, doesn't mean you can simply sit back and take it easy while God does all the work. Remember, He has given you specific talents, skills, and passions for a purpose, and He expects you to use them. While He has promised to meet your needs and ease your burdens, He will not do for you what He has equipped you to do for yourself.

You may recall how God miraculously fed the Israelites during the forty years they wandered in the wilderness, sending bread—manna—from heaven. Finally they arrived in the Promised Land, a bountiful land, fertile for growing crops.

Joshua 5:10-12 describes the last day God supplied manna:

On the evening of the fourteenth day of the month, while camped
at Gilgal on the plains of Jericho, the Israelites celebrated the
Passover. The day after the Passover, that very day, they ate some
of the produce of the land: unleavened bread and roasted grain.
The manna stopped the day after they ate this food from the land;
there was no longer any manna for the Israelites, but that year they
ate of the produce of Canaan. (NIV)

God had given them the land as a gift, but the Israelites would need to use their strength, talents, and resources to provide for themselves.

So, too, there comes a point in your spiritual growth when God will cease to spoon-feed you blessings. He wants you to stand on your own two feet, recognizing the power you have within you and the resources around you. While you absolutely must stay connected to God through prayer, you also need to be sure to ask yourself, "Have I applied all my resources to solve this problem? Or am I waiting on God to fix a dilemma that He has already given me the resources to handle?"

At times you may ask God to resolve a particular situation or change your circumstances when you should be praying for the discipline and energy to overcome them or for the wisdom to see what He is trying to teach you through them.

When we allow Him to do so, God serves as a divine parent, helping us learn how to deal with setbacks, challenges, and fears. If you will listen, He will lead, guide, and teach you. He will order your steps. And just as the relationship is strongest when a child learns to trust a parent's wisdom, you will grow closer to God as you learn to rely on His direction.

He will not necessarily always direct you to take action. In fact, God will sometimes erect roadblocks to hold you back for His purposes, and it is critical that your connection with Him be strong enough that you recognize when that happens. If you keep trying to force your way through, you will likely hurt yourself and still not get where you are trying to go.

For example, you may have invested time in a relationship that you just knew would result in marriage. Your significant other isn't interested in a long-term commitment, so you take it upon yourself to convince him that the two of you were meant to be together. Then you discover he's found someone else. Yes, it's devastating, heartbreaking. Be thankful. God has protected you by revealing the truth now rather than after you've invested even more of yourself in a hopeless situation. Although it's natural to mourn your perceived loss, you can bounce back, learn the lessons the relationship was meant to teach you, and begin healing and mentally preparing yourself for something better.

Pay attention when you feel in your spirit that a particular action is not the right one or when you simply cannot pry open a door of opportunity. Whether a relationship has ended, you've lost your job to a layoff, your business has failed, or some other disappointment has closed a door in your life, at times you will have no choice but to cease activity in a particular area. Trust that this is part of God's plan to help you grow. Rather than giving up in defeat or trying to force things to go your way, maximize your spiritual leverage by trusting that God has a strategy to take you in a new and better direction.

Closing the Gap

Focus Your Thoughts
In the face of your fears, always remember that God is with you wherever you go. He will not leave you or forsake you.

Use Your Words Wisely
When you hit a roadblock, make a habit of turning to God in prayer, seeking His wisdom and direction.

Target Your Actions
Consider an area of life in which you've been trying to force a desire into reality in your own strength. Determine to release that "burden" to God, turning your back on it for forty-eight hours. Then wait to see if He brings to mind a new solution or asks you to let that dream go, and allow Him to replace it with something better.

Energize Your Spirit

Lord, I pray for Your anointing on my life. I don't want to live my life and pursue success in my strength alone. Help me enhance the natural gifts and talents You have given me so that I can use them to the fullest. I want to rely on You and rest in the promise that You are with me. Amen.

Twenty-Five

Has "Your Way" Led to a Roadblock?

Open Your Mind to Alternative Solutions

Brian, who runs a bookstore, penned a fascinating book. But he didn't know how to go about getting it published. His dream was to land an agent who would find a publisher to fall in love with his prose. When he turned to me for advice, I directed him to the book I used to find my first agent, the *Writer's Guide to Book Editors, Publishers, and Literary Agents* by Jeff Herman. I suggested he use that resource to select five to ten agents who tend to represent works in his genre. "Then send them a query letter and follow up," I advised. "Be patient and persevere, because you

---

Portions of this chapter are adapted from Valorie Burton, The Life Enrichment Challenge, Challenge 1: "I Have a Vision for My Life That Excites and Challenges Me," January 26, 2004, www.BlackAmericaWeb.com.

will likely get lots of rejections since they receive so many inquiries on a daily basis."

Months later I talked to Brian about his book again. He had inquired of only one agent and one publisher with no response from either. Sounding dejected, he told me he guessed he didn't have my "kind of luck."

"If you want *my* kind of luck," I quipped, "maybe you should start by publishing the book yourself."

"Oh no. I don't want to do that," he said. "I want a 'real' publisher to publish my book."

But if Brian was going to insist on finding a "real" publisher to publish his book, he needed to contact more than one agent and one publisher! Otherwise, self-publishing would offer him a viable alternative. Thousands of best-selling authors began as self-published authors, including Mark Twain, John Grisham, T. D. Jakes, and Ken Blanchard, to name a few. They had the drive and boldness to take a chance on their work before anyone else would, and their initial efforts led to even greater success down the road. But Brian wanted his dream the way he wanted it. He wasn't open to alternatives, even if they might eventually lead to his ultimate objective. Several years have passed now, and his completed—but unpublished—manuscript lies on a shelf gathering dust.

Is it possible that you've made a similar mistake? Are you stuck because you insist that your vision unfold "your way"? The "my way only" syndrome can surface in any area of life. Perhaps your doctor has informed you that you need to change your diet, but you don't want to give up sugar or fried foods or salt or whatever he instructed you to do. Perhaps you've been refusing to compromise in a relationship, always insisting that your way prevail. In time you may find the relationship stalled indefinitely—or worse yet, irreparably damaged. Those who insist on their way at work garner a negative reputation and are often the first to be laid off.

Stubbornly keeping to one "ideal" path and refusing to consider alternate routes can lead you straight to a roadblock. In contrast, when you broaden your options and consider possible detours along the way, you'll discover more opportunities for reaching your goals. In many cases, the path that requires more work and offers less glamour will yield the greatest experience and success. Achieving your best possible life is a process of learning and growing. God is molding you into the person He needs you to be in order to fulfill His purpose for your life. By conquering your pride and remaining open to other means of reaching your goals, you allow God to connect you with people and teach you lessons that may lead to even greater success than you envisioned.

Oftentimes we tend to idealize the process of achieving success. We may daydream about the perfect career, the perfect relationship, or the perfect financial situation. But things rarely happen perfectly—or even in the ways we might expect or prefer. So it's crucial to keep an open mind. As we saw earlier, Brian has limited his options because his ego needs the validation of a publisher in order to feel successful. He has given more weight to the words and approval of other people than to his own passion and inner voice. In addition, he has allowed his fear of rejection to keep him from knocking on more doors.

When you focus not on your fears but on your purpose—the reason you are here on this earth at this point in time—the validation of people and organizations does not guide your decisions. When you're more concerned about having a positive impact on this world than about getting your own way, you'll discover many unexpected pathways to success.

I urge you to keep an open mind when it comes to alternative solutions or paths to your vision. God is so creative, and He can bring your vision to pass in a multitude of ways. If you find yourself stuck, pray that He'll open your eyes to a new direction you should consider.

A fundamental part of finding a pathway to success is recognizing that your life is not about you. True success doesn't mean you always get your own way or accomplish things in a way that is most pleasing to you. It's all about becoming the person God wants you to be as you realize His purpose for your life.

Sometimes God will close doors that might make it easy for you to claim the victory for yourself. He may lead you instead toward opportunities that are so obviously supernaturally directed that you could never claim credit for your achievements. People will show up in your path to help you. Opportunities will drop into your lap, seemingly out of the blue.

When your way does not seem to work, let your steps take you toward a new path, and trust that God's way will serve an even greater purpose than you had in mind.

Closing the Gap

Focus Your Thoughts

As you consider an area in which you seem to have hit a roadblock, meditate on this passage from the Bible: " 'For My thoughts are not your thoughts, nor are your ways My ways,' says the LORD. 'For as the heavens are higher than the earth, so are My ways higher than your ways, and My thoughts than your thoughts' " (Isaiah 55:8-9).

Use Your Words Wisely

Contemplate the following question and write out all the answers that come to mind: "What options have I not considered for closing the gap between where I am and where I want to be?"

Target Your Actions

Choose one of the options you noted above and see if a new pathway opens up.

Energize Your Spirit

Lord, please help me open my mind to better ideas and alternatives to "my way." Help me see when my ego, insecurities, or fears cause me to narrow my thinking and limit Your power in my life in any way. Amen.

Twenty-Six

Is It Time to Raise the Bar?

Learn from Constructive Criticism

Isn't it interesting how one person's encouragement can give you the confidence to delve deeper into your gifts and talents? Perhaps a parent, an aunt or uncle, or a friend has given you the little push you needed to explore a passion or a talent.

The seeds for my interest in writing were planted early in life, during a parent-teacher conference at Rhein Main Elementary School in Frankfurt, West Germany, where my family lived at the time. My second-grade teacher, Ms. Johnson, told my parents I was good at writing and urged them to encourage me in my poetry efforts. Ms. Johnson always raved about my early poetic "masterpieces," even sending a few off to be published in children's magazines. Here's one I remember:

I like to rip and run,
and play in the sun.

Walk and talk and
play with chalk!

Apparently I wasn't big on epic poetry. Short and sweet was my motto.

As hilarious as those early efforts seem now, Ms. Johnson effectively nurtured my passion in such a way that I always felt self-assured about my writing ability. All the way through college, I consistently earned high marks in English classes and on term papers.

So when I began studying for my master's degree in journalism in 1993, I felt more than confident that I had what it took to succeed. Imagine my shock during the first semester of graduate school when my first assignment in Dr. Workman's newswriting and reporting class was returned with red ink all over the page and a C marked at the top! *How can this be?* I thought. I even double-checked the name on the paper to make sure it was really mine.

When I asked my professor why my work had received such an underwhelming response, she informed me that my sentences were too long and complicated and my words were too big. "This is journalism," she informed me. "You need to write so that the average tenth grader can understand it. You aren't trying to impress people. You are trying to communicate and inform them." In other words, get to the point and get there as quickly and directly as possible.

She raised the bar for me in just a few short months. I thought I was good; she challenged me to be better. I had to break some longstanding habits and recondition myself to change my writing style, but the challenge was just what I needed. To this day I use the skills I learned in Dr. Workman's class not just for writing columns and books but also in preparing speeches, business letters, and proposals.

Constructive criticism can be difficult to swallow unless you embrace it as an opportunity to gain the knowledge, skills, understanding, and wisdom you need to move forward.

Most of us are aware of our strengths on at least some level, and our expertise and past success may lead us to feel exceptionally confident in particular areas of life. But we must always be willing to be challenged to reach higher and further. As motivational speaker Les Brown says, "You don't know what you don't know—and think you do." In other words, you may think you know everything you need to, but you don't. And worse yet, you don't even realize it!

So how do you know whom to listen to? How do you recognize when to heed the criticism of others as a way to grow, improve, and move closer to your vision? Here are some ways to know that someone's suggestions are worth considering:

- The person offering the criticism understands the issue, from his or her own experience, and thus has the foundation to properly assess it and offer alternatives for improvement.
- If you heed the advice, you will see positive improvement in that particular area of your life.
- Following the advice will stretch you and cause you to grow in a positive way.
- You feel God nudging you to listen and follow the advice, regardless of how you may feel about the person giving it.

Some people who prompt you to raise the bar may not do so in the nicest way. Their criticisms may feel insulting, but you must take the emotion out of your response and listen for any lessons or messages God is trying to deliver that will help you move forward. Many people miss their opportunity for growth because they are more focused on the shortcomings of the messenger than on the content of the message. In addition, people can raise the bar for you without your ever meeting them or having a conversation. By observing those who are where you'd like to be, you can find inspiration from their example and raise the bar for yourself.

Many people are held back because they never raise the bar high enough and redefine excellence for themselves. The solution is to put yourself in environments that stretch you and to surround yourself with people who will challenge you to do more and be better than you are. Proverbs tells us that "as iron sharpens iron, so one man sharpens another" (27:17, NIV). It also says, "In a multitude of counselors there is safety" (24:6). You may feel most at ease with people whose knowledge or skills are equal to yours, but if you want to grow, you need to be around people from whom you can learn. You need to spend time with individuals who, through their wisdom and expertise, can sharpen you and counsel you.

These are the people who push you closer to your vision. They give you the knowledge you need to get where you want to go. They not only challenge you to do better, they show you how. Their refusal to lightly toss you praise can be humbling and healthy. Resistance builds muscles, giving you the strength you need to push forward.

This type of useful, constructive criticism applies to more than just your professional life. In your relationships, for example, if you haven't had excellent role models, you can certainly make better choices than those you observed growing up. However, your relationships may still fall below your potential. By seeking out relationship role models—people who interact with others in a positive way—you can move past obstacles and issues you may not previously have been aware of. Just as a mentor can help you move ahead in your career, a mentor can do the same for other areas of your life.

Consider your relationships, finances, spiritual life, and eating and exercise habits. Who would you trust for constructive criticism and mentoring in each of these areas? Identify people who will stretch you and help you gain the edge to overcome the restraints that hold you back in these key areas of your life. If you can't find the right mentor among your personal friends, colleagues, or family members, consider someone who is paid to help others succeed in these areas, such as a therapist, coach, financial planner, nutritionist, or personal trainer. Seek the people you need to help you raise the bar in your life and give you the know-how to help you vault over it.

Closing the Gap

Focus Your Thoughts
Take some time to examine your life for areas in which you may have stopped actively trying to grow and improve.

Use Your Words Wisely
Keeping in mind what you learned from the exercise above, approach someone who is wiser or more experienced than you in a particular area. Ask how that person thinks you could improve, then listen closely and embrace his or her constructive criticism as an opportunity to grow stronger and better.

Target Your Actions
Consider joining a group or organization whose members offer you both the opportunity to learn from those with more experience and to mentor those with less.

Energize Your Spirit

Lord, I want to be able to accept and use constructive criticism to strengthen my skills, character, and opportunities. Please place people in my path from whom I can learn, and help me embrace the wisdom they offer. Amen.

Twenty-Seven

Are You Living in the Past or Learning from It?

Glean the Lessons, Then Move On

One of the most effective means of improving your success rate is to take some time to review your performance. Professionals in a variety of fields use this process to stretch and grow. Football teams and coaches review footage from their games so they can determine what successful actions to repeat and what ineffective moves to eliminate. Singers often evaluate recordings of their performances in much the same way. Speakers videotape their presentations, then watch to see where they lost the attention of their audiences and where they effectively drove home their messages.

In a similar way, your past provides a tremendous opportunity for growth if you diligently seek to learn from your experiences, mistakes, failures, and successes. Sometimes you have to dig fairly deep to answer the question, What's the lesson in that experience? Although it can be difficult to evaluate your own performance, it is immensely helpful in determining ways to improve and laying out a new course of action.

One powerful form of coaching—called "coactive coaching"—is designed for this express purpose. In their book *Co-Active Coaching,* Laura Whitworth, Henry Kimsey-House, and Phil Sandahl describe the connection between action and learning:

> These two forces, action and learning, combine to create change. Because the notion of *action* that moves the client forward is so central to the purpose of coaching, we make "forward" a verb and say that one of the purposes of coaching is to "forward the action" of the client. The other force at work in the human change process is *learning.* Learning is not simply a by-product of action, it is an equal and complementary force. The learning generates new resourcefulness, expanded possibilities, stronger muscles for change.*

Whether or not you have a personal coach, the key to closing the gaps in your life is moving past the surface fluff and discovering what it will take to get where you want to be. It's all part of the process of personal growth, and although a coach tries to help you move forward toward your vision, the real value is not always in the action. What you learn through the process of taking action can be much more vital to your overall growth.

For example, I recall one project in which I procrastinated to an appalling extent. Eventually, the knowledge of the incomplete work weighed so

---

* Laura Whitworth, Henry Kimsey-House, and Phil Sandahl, *Co-Active Coaching* (Palo Alto, CA: Davies-Black, 1998), 5.

heavily on me that I began to feel sick. I finally became fed up with my own inaction and moved forward. You know what? I thoroughly enjoyed the project once I really got into it! When I finished, I was ready to take on another.

As I reviewed the experience to determine what I could do differently the second time around, I realized that I had allowed myself to be overwhelmed by the immensity of the project and couldn't see that it would get done one minute at a time—if I would just get started! Once I broke it down into manageable pieces, I was able to make consistent, effective progress. This lesson has been a major source of professional growth for me.

When you face roadblocks—and when you overcome them—take some time to evaluate your actions and determine what works for you and what doesn't.

Be careful, however, about allowing the past to dominate your thoughts. When you are constantly looking over your shoulder and into your past—recounting your experiences, imagining how things could have gone differently, wishing for a different outcome—you cannot see the new opportunities that lie before you.

Have you been dwelling in the past rather than simply learning from it? Perhaps you reminisce about your successes and the "good old days." You spend your time reliving joyous memories and mourning the passing of relationships that have since faded away. Or maybe your past was filled with turmoil, pain, abuse, or a series of difficulties. Unfair or unpleasant childhood experiences have shaped how you view the world and the people who live in it. Or perhaps your thoughts are filled with regrets over a tumultuous marriage or with resentment about injustice or discrimination that prevented you from fulfilling your potential at a previous job.

Often we don't even realize we're making decisions based in fears and insecurities born of past negative experiences. When Stuart was just three years old, his parents divorced, and his father moved more than a thousand miles away. To Stuart's detriment, his father seemed unable to distinguish between his severed relationship with his wife and his ongoing relationship with his son. He rarely called, even on birthdays. Stuart's mother had to take legal action to obtain child support. Eventually Stuart's father remarried and had more children. Stuart naturally resented the attention the other children received.

By the time he reached adulthood Stuart was seething with deep-rooted anger and resentment toward his father. Those toxic emotions spilled into his other relationships. He couldn't believe anyone would stay in a relationship with him, so he would never fully commit. At age thirty-four, he faced a crossroads: His girlfriend of five years was ready to move on. It seemed clear that her relationship with Stuart would not lead to marriage, and she was not interested in a permanent dating relationship. Stuart believed she was "the one," but his fear of vulnerability was simply too much for him. He let her slip away. Six years later he is still filled with regret. He's only now coming to realize what a grip his past has on his present perspective.

Are you, like Stuart, allowing the past to dictate rather than merely inform your current life? Have you found yourself thinking or saying any of the following?

- "I tried that before and it didn't work. I'm not doing it again."
- "But you don't understand. I was hurt/abused/mistreated. Because of my past, I can't behave any differently. This is just how I am now."
- "I'll never be that happy again."

- "I know everything I need to know."
- "I can't let anyone into my life. I don't want to be hurt again."
- "You can't trust anybody."
- "No one will ever accept me after all I've done and the mistakes I've made."

If these or similar thoughts are keeping you tied to the past, it's time to shift your attention to the present and recenter your thoughts on God's Word. The apostle Paul in his letter to the Philippians, wrote, "One thing I do, forgetting those things which are behind and reaching forward to those things which are ahead, I press toward the goal for the prize of the upward call of God in Christ Jesus" (3:13-14).

Learn from your past, but don't let it control you. Take advantage of the opportunity you have right now to transform and enjoy your life.

Closing the Gap

Focus Your Thoughts
Think back on the past week and note one thing you would do differently if you could. Now forgive yourself for that mistake and set your sights on the week ahead.

Use Your Words Wisely
When you are tempted to dwell on the past in conversation, refocus your words on the present and your future. Certainly, it is appropriate to discuss the past and reminisce sometimes, but do not allow your conversations to be dominated by "what was."

Target Your Actions

Today, identify a milestone worth celebrating. Whether it's a new attitude or a new job, acknowledge your progress.

Energize Your Spirit

Lord, I thank You that You have given me hope and a future. Open my mind and heart to learn the lessons You are teaching me so that I can grow into the person I need to be. Show me how to take action and make adjustments to my actions based on Your Word and my unique path in life. Help me live in the moment and fully enjoy my daily life. Amen.

Twenty-Eight

Are You Ready to Play a Bigger Game?

Prepare to Move to the Next Level

Have you been dreaming of bigger things—running a marathon, pursuing a more rewarding career, nurturing a more fulfilling relationship, developing a deeper connection with God—yet find yourself settling for what you have, intimidated by what it would take to accomplish your vision? It's natural to think small when fear is controlling your decisions. Rather than imagining a great relationship, you think about just keeping the peace. Rather than planning for financial abundance, you settle for financial survival. Rather than going for what you really want, you downsize your dream.

Fear of rejection, failure, success, or inadequacy—all of these can contribute to "playing a smaller game" than you are capable of.

Consider these words your wake-up call! It's time to stop shrinking from your potential and start fulfilling it. Despite your fear, I challenge you to step up to the plate and play a bigger game. It's easy to succeed when you aim low, but when you aim high and play a bigger game, you have the opportunity to truly show what you are made of. A bigger game challenges you to do more and be more than you have in the past. What will that require?

First, you'll have to use the gifts you've been given. If you're not applying your natural gifts and abilities every day, you are living far beneath your potential. Your purpose in this world is to use your gifts to serve others, and playing a bigger game means harnessing every one of your God-given talents and skills toward that goal.

A second requirement for moving to the next level is to play by bigger rules. For example, those who seek financial freedom don't make decisions by the same rules as those who seek merely to survive financially. A person who desires healthy relationships doesn't play by the same rules as someone who is always looking for "drama." A person who aims to be fit and healthy doesn't have the same daily habits as someone who isn't serious about his or her health. When you make the shift to overcome your fear and play a bigger game, you'll need to play by a bigger (and better) set of rules.

Third, a bigger game requires a bigger team. Athletes who move from high-school or college sports into professional sports suddenly gain access to a huge team of specialists whose role is to help them achieve peak performance. Similarly, when you step up to the next level, you need to broaden your connections and seek the help of others. On a bigger playing field, you can't win by yourself. Whether you need a counselor to help you improve your relationships, a coach to help you build your business or accelerate your career, friends to pray for you and support you, a once-a-week housekeeper to give you more time for other priorities, or an expert to help you learn a new skill, be sure to have the kind of people on your team who will help you win. Do they think on the level on which you need them to think? Can they see your vision? And just as important, are they on board with your vision? Do they have the skills to meet the demands of a bigger game? We'll delve further into the basics of building a good team in the next chapter, but for now, remember that having a team supporting you will decrease your risk of failure and, in the process, lower your level of fear.

As we've discussed throughout this book, fear is a thread woven through every restraint that threatens to hold you back. You may find yourself held back by the fear that you won't succeed at the next level. It's tempting to remain where you are; it's comfortable because you've learned to be successful at that level. There's no sense of excitement or challenge, but at least you know what to expect.

Let me share with you the secret to overcoming that fear, the fourth requirement for playing a bigger game: Be willing to fail.

That is the only way to experience success at a higher level. The risk of failure will never go away. It's your tolerance for it that will give you the perseverance you need to succeed. And when you fail, it is critical that you learn from your disappointment and mistakes.

Your tolerance for failure will also pay off in other ways. As you begin living life at a higher level, not allowing your fear to hold you back, new opportunities will suddenly appear. Embrace these as the fruits of your fearlessness! A bigger game pays off in a bigger way.

Rather than playing it safe and netting results that are below your potential, step up to the next level so that you can reap the rewards of living life to the fullest, being your best you, and going for what you *truly* want.

Closing the Gap

Focus Your Thoughts
Are your plans expansive enough to be in line with your divinely ordained destiny? Meditate on these words: "A man's heart plans his way, but the LORD directs his steps" (Proverbs 16:9).

Use Your Words Wisely
Write down in vivid detail what the next level looks like in each of the five key areas of your life—your relationships, career, finances and resources, physical health and environments, and spiritual life.

Target Your Actions
Choose one area of your life in which fear has been keeping you at a level beneath your potential. Perhaps you will ask for a raise, increase your rates if you are self-employed, start writing that book or play you've been day-dreaming about, get rid of the junk food in your diet, or take a new approach to your relationships. Whatever it is, identify one step you can take in the next twenty-four hours—and then do it.

Energize Your Spirit
God, help me step fully into the next level in my life. Help me see the bigger possibilities You have planned for me, and empower me to break free of any habits that discourage me from fulfilling my potential. Amen.

Twenty-Nine

Are You Trying to Go It Alone?

Enlist the Help of a Winning Personal Team

There seems to be a misconception in our society about seeking help. Somehow we have the notion that those who are strong don't need help. Independence means "I don't need anybody else." We associate "needing" people with being weak.

For a healthy person, nothing could be further from the truth. The help of others not only is a blessing, but it can also strengthen your position as you close the gaps in your life. Despite appearances, successful people don't win in isolation. They have a successful team supporting them each step of the way.

Great entertainers, for example, don't become great on their own. Acting and voice coaches, choreographers, agents, publicists, makeup artists, and producers are just a few of the professionals who contribute significantly to the success of entertainers' performances and careers. Without an excellent team, they wouldn't be able to perform as effectively or create the opportunities that allow them to shine.

The same is true for you. In every area of life, you can benefit from having a team whose gifts, talents, and experiences will help you meet your goals. That doesn't mean you have to share the details of your life with everyone. It simply requires a willingness to learn from those who have a proven record of success in the area in which you seek to be successful. For example, if you are married, having a wise mentor in your life who serves as a role model is a very wise move. You will also want to surround yourself with friends who pray for you and encourage you to keep a positive perspective about married life. If your goal is to lose forty pounds, your team might include a friend who also wants to pursue a healthier lifestyle, a doctor and/or nutritionist who advises you on a plan of action, and a trainer who develops a workout plan for you.

Building a team may also involve delegating certain aspects of your to-do list so that you can concentrate on priorities that further your key purposes. God teaches the principle of delegating in the book of Exodus when Moses's father-in-law, Jethro, cautioned Moses and advised him to stop taking on every dispute that the people brought to him:

> What you are doing is not good. You and these people who come to
> you will only wear yourselves out. The work is too heavy for you;
> you cannot handle it alone. Listen now to me and I will give you
> some advice, and may God be with you. You must be the people's
> representative before God and bring their disputes to him. Teach
> them the decrees and laws, and show them the way to live and the
> duties they are to perform. But select capable men from all the

people—men who fear God, trustworthy men who hate dishonest gain—and appoint them as officials over thousands, hundreds, fifties and tens. Have them serve as judges for the people at all times, but have them bring every difficult case to you; the simple cases they can decide themselves. That will make your load lighter, because they will share it with you. If you do this and God so commands, you will be able to stand the strain, and all these people will go home satisfied. (Exodus 18:17-23, NIV)

Perhaps the idea of asking for help simply never occurred to you before, but my guess is, if you haven't begun gathering a support team, it's probably because the idea of asking others for help makes you uneasy. Let me encourage you to take some time to figure out why. Might any of the following reasons explain your discomfort?

- You're afraid of rejection. It seems easier to battle through on your own than to face the possibility that someone may turn down your request for help.
- You don't think anyone else can do what you do, or do it as well.
- You want all the accolades. You don't want to share the spotlight if and when you succeed. Instead, you want people to know you did it all yourself. It's called pride, ego, self-centeredness.
- You aren't connected with the right kind of people.
- You're too shy, embarrassed, ashamed, or proud to tell anyone about your needs.
- You believe that asking for help is a sign of weakness.
- You believe you're not far enough along in your plans to involve other people.

Here are some points to remember when you find yourself shrinking behind some of these excuses:

- You are more effective when you don't try to do everything yourself but instead focus on what you do best and allow others to do the same.

- Forming a team and delegating are two of the keys to preserving your energy and enhancing your overall well-being.

- Let go of your need to get all the credit, remembering that your purpose and your life are about more than you. A greater purpose is fulfilled when you allow others into the process and give them the opportunity to learn and grow from it.

- Seeking help sometimes forces you outside your comfort zone, allowing you to connect with new people. Often these individuals will serve a greater purpose in your life.

- God is trying to stretch you, to help you move beyond your fear of rejection, your shy or timid personality, or your issues of pride. As you follow His guidance and reach further than you feel comfortable doing, you'll often break through what's holding you back from greater levels of success.

Whatever the reason for your hesitation, let me encourage you to reconsider your position and start asking for help. Now I'm not suggesting that you seek handouts or ask people to grant you favors that you wouldn't be willing to return if the situation were reversed. Instead, I am suggesting that you consider what kind of assistance you need to move to the next level of your life and who is best equipped to provide it.

The following questions may help you pinpoint the type of help you might ask for and who to approach:

1. In what areas of your life are you facing uncertainty or confusion about how to proceed? Who might be able to give you direction?

2. Are there emotional barriers you still need to work through? Who might be able to help you through the process? A trusted friend? A counselor? Your pastor?

3. What expertise are you lacking that would help you close the gap? Who has that knowledge, and how can you get these people on your team? This might include experts such as a personal trainer, financial planner, coach, or mentor.

4. Who could hold you accountable to meet your goals and/or change your habits?

5. Are the resources needed to close the gap beyond your reach? Who could help you access the right resources?

You may already have a team in place, even if you haven't thought of these people in those terms. However, you need to be sure you aren't relying on someone who is more of a hindrance than a help. Take some time to review the characteristics of people you consider to be part of your team, in both your personal and professional life. Are those you've turned to for support truly helping, or are they holding you back? Are their words edifying and constructive, or do they tend to be negative and discouraging? Does their influence make you better and stronger, or do they lead you in unhealthy directions?

Just as important as having the right team is being willing to serve others with your skills and resources. When you demonstrate a willingness to help those who cross your path, people will reciprocate. When you sow into the lives of others, you strengthen your future, making the essential connections that will lead to your success.

Closing the Gap

Focus Your Thoughts

In each of the five key areas of your life—your relationships, career, finances and resources, physical health and environments, and spiritual life—think of one way in which you could benefit from the help of one or more people.

Use Your Words Wisely

Based on the needs you identified above, make a list of people who could help you close the gaps in your life. Then ask at least two of them for the help you need.

Target Your Actions

Identify at least one person who might benefit from the skills and talents with which God has blessed you. Offer your support in a specific, tangible way.

Energize Your Spirit

Dear God, please open my eyes to the areas in which I need help. Grant me the wisdom to know who to ask and the integrity never to ask out of selfishness, laziness, or impure motives. Give me the discernment to know when to offer my help to others. God, I believe You will bring me into contact with the right people at the right time, and I thank You for the people You have so graciously placed in my life to help me become all that You want me to be. Amen.

Thirty

Do You Know How to Ask for What You Want?

Articulate Your Needs or Concerns Effectively

The area in which people most often seek my advice by e-mail is relationships. Many people find themselves frustrated with spouses, children, parents, siblings, significant others, co-workers, friends, and neighbors. Some harbor resentment for being wronged in some way, yet in many cases the other person has no idea that a grudge is being held against him, or if he does know, he's unsure why. In many of these instances, the frustrated person has not clearly expressed her expectations for the relationship. For some reason—usually based in fear—she has not truthfully or effectively articulated her needs and desires. Then she finds herself stuck in a vicious cycle of disagreements and unhappiness.

To reach your goals—in business, relationships, finances, or any area of life—you must be able to say what needs to be said and to ask for what you want. No matter how strong your passion or how terrific your ideas, if you won't speak up for yourself or can't communicate effectively, you'll find yourself stuck at a level beneath your potential. And the longer you hesitate, the more frustration and stress will build up inside you.

Do you need to speak to someone about a request but don't know how to begin? Do you find yourself tongue-tied when you approach others— too nervous, insecure, or doubtful to ask for the help you need? Perhaps you feel it's time for a raise, or you want to improve a foundering relationship. Before asking for what you want, it is critically important to determine how to articulate your needs or concerns most effectively.

The following questions will help you develop a strategy to ask for what you want and move closer to your vision:

1. What do I want to happen as a result of the conversation? Envision, clearly and specifically, the desired outcome of your conversation. What result are you seeking? Do you want a raise? How much more do you feel is reasonable? What amount would you be willing to settle for? Do you want the other person or both of you to take some specific action? Be sure you know exactly what you want accomplished and when. Do you desire to better understand where the other person is coming from? Do you want to put an end to a specific behavior or situation? Know precisely what you want to accomplish, and guide the conversation toward that specific course of action.

2. What is the most important message I want to communicate? In most situations you'll need to explain the why behind your request. Why is your request for a raise reasonable? Why do you want the other person to change a specific behavior or take a particular action? But restrict your reasons to only the most important factors. The more succinctly you can explain your points, the more likely it is that you will reach a successful outcome. Resist the temptation to bring up secondary issues that aren't truly essential or relevant to what you are trying to communicate. Otherwise, the other person may be distracted by your "rabbit trails," and the conversation may never get back on track—leaving you frustrated and unsuccessful in your bid for change.

3. Am I focused on content or emotion? Any issue of importance to you will naturally involve strong feelings. If you are seeking a raise, it's possible that the topic has been on your mind for a long time. Perhaps you have some frustration about how hard you work and feel that your compensation is not fair or adequate. However, emotional communication is usually counterproductive. If you allow the frustration of your emotions to affect your choice of words, you will likely sabotage the success of the conversation. Practice speaking in a neutral tone so that you build bridges for open communication rather than building walls that will make the other person defensive. Stay focused on the content and facts that support your request. Similarly, when you're seeking help from someone who would make a great member of your personal team, it's certainly appropriate to let your enthusiasm for your vision shine through. But remember to be clear about what you want through the content of the conversation.

4. What is the right time and place? Be sure you choose the optimal time and place for your conversation. If it is a professional matter, schedule a meeting with the appropriate person, but be sensitive to other obligations and appointments that person may have. When you need to approach a loved one to ask for a change in behavior or to discuss a topic about which he or she may be touchy, do so when the atmosphere is neutral. Refrain from raising important issues during an argument, when your loved one has had a challenging day, or anytime emotions are running high. Attempting a serious conversation with your spouse or family member during his or her favorite television program might not be the best plan either. Select a time when you both are in the right frame of mind and free of distractions.

5. What is the other person's perspective? You may feel passionate about what you want, but be sure to consider the other person's wants and needs as well. During the course of the conversation, ask for feedback. Be sure to listen rather than plowing ahead with your agenda. Ask questions to make sure you understand the other person's thinking. Try to remain open to alternative suggestions, but don't lose sight of the goal you identified in question 1. Once you understand the other person's perspective, use that information to settle on a mutually agreed upon outcome and bring closure to the conversation.

Knowing how to ask for what you want is a powerful skill. It can save you time, open doors of opportunity, and move you forward more quickly to close the gaps in your life. Even God tells us throughout the Bible that we must ask Him for what we want. The apostle Paul urged his readers, "Let your requests be made known to God" (Philippians 4:6). Jesus promised, "And whatever things you ask in prayer, believing, you will receive" (Matthew 21:22). The writer of the book of James warns us, "You do not have because you do not ask" (4:2).

Clearly, God wants us to approach Him with our requests, dreams, and desires. The key is to ask in faith and with pure motives, seeking only those things that are pleasing to God and that will help you fulfill your divinely ordained vision.

Closing the Gap

Focus Your Thoughts

In what areas of your life have you been hesitating to ask God or other people for what you want?

Use Your Words Wisely

Write out, in vivid detail, the change or outcome you want to see in at least one of the key areas of your life—your relationships, career, finances and resources, physical health and environments, and spiritual life.

Target Your Actions

Set a deadline to resolve this concern, then speak up for yourself and ask for what you want!

Energize Your Spirit

Lord, Your Word says that if I lack wisdom, I should ask for it in faith, without doubting, and You will give it to me. I believe that You will fulfill that promise, and so I ask You now to give me the wisdom to know what to ask for, who to ask, and when. Amen.

Thirty-One

How Has God Uniquely Equipped You?

Tap into the Power of Your Skills, Talents, and Experiences

Recently I tuned in to the *Suze Orman Show,* a television program on CNBC hosted by personal finance expert and author Suze Orman. This particular show included a talented, twenty-three-year-old woman who was struggling with her finances. A recent college graduate with a music degree, she was earning about $16,000 per year as an administrative assistant in Los Angeles while awaiting an opportunity to launch a music career. With more expenses than income, she admitted that her parents were paying her student loans as well as her health and car insurance. She was even charging food on her credit card—and her balance now totaled $7,500. Her face and body language revealed that she didn't just feel badly about her financial situation, she was beginning to lose hope. She didn't feel she had many options, and everything about her seemed to indicate that she was bereft of confidence.

When Suze invited her to sing, however, this young woman was transformed. Complete confidence consumed her as she sang two verses of "Amazing Grace," her soulful voice filling the airwaves. Clearly, she had both passion and talent.

"When did you last write a song or perform publicly?" Suze asked.

"Well," the young woman replied, "it's been about a year, I guess."

The longer she went without performing or writing, the more frustrated she had become and the more hope she lost. But, as Suze pointed out, the same confidence that empowered the young woman to respond on the spot to an impromptu request could be tapped as a resource for digging her way out of her financial hole. In fact, focusing on alternative ways to make money using her voice would not only build her strength by giving her an outlet to perform, but it could also provide her with the additional income she needed to close the gap in her financial circumstances.

As this woman's story illustrates, we are weakest when we don't make sufficient room in our lives for our purpose, passion, and values. When we remain idle, wasting our effort on talking about our goals but never moving forward on them, we actually deplete our energy. A similar problem occurs when we act in ways that don't reflect our individuality, trying to duplicate the approach of someone else or follow another's path to success. When we don't embrace our own uniqueness, we demonstrate a lack of faith in God's ability to work through us. We are weakened by choosing not to be ourselves.

On the other hand, we gain strength from taking steps that fulfill our purpose, passion, and values because such actions embody the essence of who you and I were created to be. As I've mentioned before, God has given each of us specific talents, skills, and passions for a purpose, and He expects us to use them. Whenever we take actions that are in line with what we were created and anointed to do, we will experience joy. Through that experience of joy, we'll be reenergized—and power will be released into our lives. "The joy of the LORD is your strength," Nehemiah 8:10 tells us.

The story of David and Goliath in the Old Testament book of 1 Samuel demonstrates the urgency of paying attention to how God has uniquely equipped each of us. David and Goliath's encounter occurred during a standoff between the armies of the Israelites and the Philistines. Goliath, a fighting Philistine champion who was over nine feet tall, had challenged the Israelites to send out someone to fight him. "If he is able to fight and kill me," the giant proposed, "we will become your subjects; but if I overcome him and kill him, you will become our subjects and serve us" (1 Samuel 17:9, NIV). The Bible tells us that "on hearing the Philistine's words, Saul and all the Israelites were dismayed and terrified (verse 11, NIV). For forty days Goliath repeated his challenge, but apparently the Israelites were too paralyzed with fear to respond.

This is when young David arrived on the scene, having come to visit his soldier brothers. David recognized two very important factors: First, while others saw a giant when they looked at Goliath, David saw a mere mortal with mortal abilities and limitations. When he heard Goliath's arrogant proposal, David asked, "Who is this uncircumcised Philistine that he should defy the armies of the living God?" (verse 26, NIV). David knew that if God was on his side, he needed nothing more than the abilities that had already been placed in him.

Second, he recognized the value of his own unique experiences in defeating the enemy. When David stepped forward to accept Goliath's challenge, Saul objected, "You are not able to go out against this Philistine and fight him; you are only a boy, and he has been a fighting man from his youth" (verse 33, NIV). David responded by telling Saul about his experiences protecting his father's sheep against lion and bear attacks. "Your servant has killed both the lion and the bear; this uncircumcised Philistine will be like one of them, because he has defied the armies of the living God," the young man declared. "The LORD who delivered me from the paw of the lion and the paw of the bear will deliver me from the hand of this Philistine" (verses 36-37, NIV).

Being a shepherd may not have seemed as noble and important as King Saul's position, but David was anointed, and his work as a shepherd was preparation for his success.

As he made ready to confront the giant, David remained true to who he was at that point in his life, rejecting royal armor for a simpler approach. Let's read what happened:

Saul said to David, "Go, and the LORD be with you."

Then Saul dressed David in his own tunic. He put a coat of armor on him and a bronze helmet on his head. David fastened on his sword over the tunic and tried walking around, because he was not used to them.

"I cannot go in these," he said to Saul, "because I am not used to them." So he took them off. Then he took his staff in his hand, chose five smooth stones from the stream, put them in the pouch of his shepherd's bag and, with his sling in his hand, approached the Philistine [Goliath]....

As the Philistine moved closer to attack him, David ran quickly toward the battle line to meet him. Reaching into his bag and taking out a stone, he slung it and struck the Philistine on the forehead. The stone sank into his forehead, and he fell facedown on the ground.

So David triumphed over the Philistine with a sling and a stone; without a sword in his hand he struck down the Philistine and killed him. (verses 37-40,48-50, NIV)

David turned his strength as a shepherd into strength as a warrior. The principles and abilities needed were the same, though the circumstances were different. He had to appreciate his past experiences, which had shaped his character and strength, in order to see that he could win by simply being himself.

Just like David, you are uniquely equipped for the battles you face. God has given you the skills and talents you need to break through obstacles and fulfill your purpose. In addition, He has directed you to experiences that have prepared you for whatever lies ahead.

Embracing the experiences that have shaped you and expressing your individuality by exercising your unique skills and talents gives you the freedom to succeed in the way that works best for you. Remember, God does not necessarily call those who are qualified. Instead, He qualifies those He calls. A major source of your strength is derived from the fact that God called you, and whether or not you acknowledge it, He has equipped you for whatever He has called you to do. If you deny your unique qualifications, you are choosing to forgo your own strength.

You are strongest when you embody the person God created you to be. You possess the strength to move forward, if only you will dig deep for the lessons you have learned and the character you have developed.

Closing the Gap

Focus Your Thoughts

Think about all the ways God has uniquely equipped you to experience victory in the battles you face.

Use Your Words Wisely

Make a list of your unique gifts and talents, as well as the personal experiences that have helped define and refine your character.

Target Your Actions

Identify a new avenue for using your talent to help others.

Energize Your Spirit

Lord, help me appreciate my own uniqueness and use it to maximize my impact. I pray for Your anointing on me as I pursue Your unique purpose and path for my life. Help me resist the temptation to be like others and instead seek ways to allow my unique successes and failures, abilities and disabilities to be used in ways that glorify You. Amen.

Thirty-Two

How Do You Deal with Naysayers?

Counteract the Negative Messages Others Send Your Way

Theresa was justifiably excited. She had just reached a milestone in her vision: completing her associate of arts degree. Now she was on her way to a four-year university to earn her bachelor's degree in nursing so she could achieve her career goal of becoming a registered nurse. Working full time and attending classes in the evenings posed a challenge, but she was up for it. She was determined to close the gap on her career potential as well as her desired income.

But at a time when she should have been free to celebrate the milestone of earning her two-year degree, Theresa's joy was muted by the reality that her family members couldn't manage to say anything positive about her progress. None of them had attended college themselves, and a few seemed jealous of her success. Others accused her of believing she was better than everyone else. She determined to persevere despite the lack of support, but her feelings about her achievements were bittersweet.

As Theresa learned in such a painful way, sometimes the people we would most expect to support our efforts do just the opposite. Dealing with naysayers—whether they actively work to discourage you or simply withhold their approval—can be confusing, frustrating, and discouraging. But if you refuse to allow them to steer you off course, you can successfully counteract their negativity.

The first thing to do when you encounter naysayers is to mentally, verbally, and actively recommit yourself to your vision. Don't allow the disapproval or jealousy of others to dissuade you from pursuing a clear, compelling, God-inspired vision for your life.

The second key to counteracting the effects of someone else's negative words is to withstand the temptation to take their comments personally. When others discourage you from making positive progress, it usually indicates an underlying issue in their own lives. Remember, most people view life from a perspective tainted by their own insecurities, negative experiences, and motives. Seek to understand rather than judge, but at the same time, pay attention to how the negativity of others affects your choices in life.

Linda, a wife, mother, and business owner, allowed naysayers to hold her back from losing weight. In our coaching sessions she often spoke of needing to get on an exercise program, but she continually failed to follow through on her plans to begin a regular exercise regimen. After a few sessions, we probed her intentions further. Her words did not match her actions, and her excuses of not having enough time simply did not ring true. She was an attractive woman but had gained weight over the years and was beginning to have some health problems. When I probed her resistance to doing something about it, she admitted that many women in her community seemed to be jealous of the success of her business and of her high-achieving husband and children. "When I gained weight," she said, "people seemed to like me better. I think it was because I now had a flaw in their eyes. They were nicer and less judgmental. I want to lose the weight for me, but if I lose it, I'll attract attention that I don't want."

Through talking it out and journaling, Linda came to the conclusion that she was not willing to allow people who did not like her for who she was to dictate the state of her health. She could forgo their "friendships" in order to get her health back on track.

In my first book, *Rich Minds, Rich Rewards,* I wrote about the importance of putting yourself in the other person's shoes, especially when that person is behaving negatively toward you. It doesn't mean that you approve of that person's behavior; it simply provides you the opportunity to look at the situation from his or her perspective. Often the people closest to you resist changes in your life because they feel left behind, jealous, or even frustrated with their own circumstances. Rather than being inspired by your example, they become defensive and see you as a target for their resentment toward life. Once you recognize this, you can respond with empathy rather than with anger, bitterness, or hurt.

If you resist the urge to argue or to respond with your own negative comments, you may be able to turn things around. Strive to find a point of connection with the other person by sharing your purpose for pursuing your goals. Then shift the focus to the other person by asking about his or her dreams and goals. People who are unsupportive often have not discovered or pursued their own life purpose. Invite them to join you on the journey to a richer life, and offer your support. At the same time, clearly state that you'd like their support. It may sound simple, but sometimes all our loved ones need is to hear that their encouragement and presence matter to us. Asking them to play a role on your support team can keep people connected to you at a time when they may be worried that you are growing apart. If people you really care about are unsupportive, let them know it bothers you not to have them on your side, and ask if they will change their attitude. Be clear that, as much as you would like their support, if they decline to offer it, you will be disappointed but not deterred.

If you persevere on your path, the courage and faith you exhibit may in time inspire those naysayers to seek change in their own lives. You have the opportunity to lead by example by breaking through the fears and obstacles that have held you back. Your example of stepping out in faith may help someone else eliminate his or her own fears. So don't give up on your negative friends and loved ones; instead, pray that they will experience a change from the inside out. You may be pleasantly surprised by the results of your positive example and the power of prayer.

While encounters with some naysayers may be unavoidable, you can minimize the amount of negativity feeding into your life by being selective about your relationships. The sheer excitement of doing something new and challenging can prompt you to tell too many people about your goals. But not everyone needs to know your plans, because not everyone has your best interests at heart. Practice discretion and protect your vision by sharing it only with those you trust.

At the same time, you'll want to be sure you have a number of positive people on your support team to help counteract any negativity from others. When you're feeling down because someone isn't offering support or is actively discouraging you, call a member of your personal team to seek positive, balanced feedback. Knowing that at least one person is in your corner rooting for you will help offset the effects of others' disapproval.

In addition to relying on the members of your support team, surround yourself with people who are pursuing their purpose and vision in life. The positive and inspiring energy of like-minded people can provide the encouragement you need to keep moving forward.

Closing the Gap

Focus Your Thoughts

When others belittle your positive efforts and progress, refuse to allow their negative words to change your mind about the vision God has ordained for you. Instead, center your thoughts on Jesus's instruction in Matthew 5:16: "Let your light so shine before men, that they may see your good works and glorify your Father in heaven."

Use Your Words Wisely

Think of someone you know who may be struggling in the pursuit of his or her own vision. Offer words of support and encouragement today. You'll be surprised how focusing on someone else in positive terms will help fuel your own passion.

Target Your Actions

Identify one or two people who can be a positive force in countering the negativity of the naysayers in your life. Ask if you can count on them to encourage you when the weight of others' discouragement becomes heavy.

Energize Your Spirit

Lord, I believe that the vision You have for every area of my life will surely come at an appointed time, if I keep my eyes on it and continue to move toward it. I pray a special blessing on those who would discourage me, that they may come to know Your vision for their lives and pursue it. I pray that You will transform their hearts and minds so that they will seek to edify and encourage those around them. Please bring into my life the right people to encourage me when I am feeling low. Amen.

Thirty-Three

Do You Need an Updated Road Map?

Ask Yourself, "What's Next?"

Twelve years into his career, Chris created a clear, compelling vision of a company he would build from the ground up. His powerful dream pulled him forward, and within five years, his vision for a multimillion-dollar business had become a reality. What Chris hadn't anticipated was that within a short time of realizing his dream, the excitement began to fade. He asked himself, "Now what?"

As I coach and speak, I find that Chris's dilemma is not uncommon. Clients and audience members often mention that they've attained the level they had envisioned for themselves in their careers, and they've also

---

Portions of this chapter are adapted from Valorie Burton's *Rich Minds, Rich Rewards* e-newsletter, June 1, 2002.

accomplished many of the objectives they had set for their personal lives. Sometimes they note that they've achieved more than they ever dreamed possible. Having reached their goals and fulfilled their dreams, they now find themselves looking toward the future and asking, "What now? I've accomplished what I set out to do, and I no longer have a dream propelling me forward. What more do I want?"

Whether you have found success in business, career, family, relationships, or your spiritual life, at some point you may find yourself asking similar questions. It's possible that you find yourself frustrated and floundering because you've already followed the route highlighted on your existing road map. You've passed all the significant milestones you anticipated and maybe made a few unexpected discoveries along the way. In other words, you had a vision, and with God's help, you brought it to life. You've achieved a certain level of success, and now you're wondering, "What's next?"

Take this as your cue to create an updated road map, anticipating unexplored opportunities waiting to be discovered. The following questions will help you chart a new course toward success.

1. What have I always wanted to do but haven't done yet? We all have dreams that lie dormant, waiting for us to bring them to life. In the past they may have been overshadowed by other more urgent dreams, but now the time is right for them to become reality. Maybe you long to own a house on the beach, go on a safari in Africa, or write the novel that's been percolating in the back of your mind. Perhaps you've noticed a particular need in your community that sparks your passion, such as assistance for the homeless or literacy programs for struggling children. Even if these dreams have little to do with your previous success, don't smother them with fears or hesitation. Remember, everything that exists in our lives begins with a thought. Begin thinking about the dreams you want to bring to life. Consider what you've already accomplished through turning your thoughts into actions and letting your actions propel you toward success.

2. What could I do that would make my work more meaningful? One reason your professional life may seem boring and stagnant is because your work, and the purpose behind it, has never changed. As you gain new experiences, insights, influence, contacts, and wisdom, you have the opportunity to apply these intellectual assets to your work.

When I moved to Dallas in late 1994, Laura Miller was a journalist on a mission, often serving as a thorn in the side of local politicians, the city council, and the mayor. A wife and mom, she was relentless in her research and criticism on issues in her community. Not everyone agreed with her perspective, but everyone seemed to be talking about the topics she addressed. Then in 1998 she decided to stop writing about the problems she perceived and start tackling them directly. She ran for—and won—a seat on the Dallas City Council. The same spark that heated up the pages of the newspaper she worked for now heated up city hall. Today Ms. Miller is the mayor of Dallas. Her knowledge of the city, politics, and the key players in the community was sharpened during her work as a journalist covering city issues. That same knowledge and passion serve her effectively today.

Ms. Miller's story offers just one example of transferring an area of interest or expertise across careers. Perhaps you have skills, passion, or knowledge that has prepared you for a leap to a new area. It could be a lateral move within the company you work for, a career change that allows you to use your experiences in a new way, or a new venture as a volunteer for a worthwhile organization that could benefit from the unique perspective you offer.

3. How could I use my influence to have a positive impact on others? We all have influence on some level. As you have progressed in your career or business, you have expanded your network and your potential influence on others. In what ways could you have a positive impact on those in your sphere of influence—fellow members of the PTA, your family, your professional network, your customers? Think of the people you have access to because of your position or your involvement in particular organizations and groups. Then consider how God wants those people to be influenced as a result of interacting with you.

In 2001 I started a weekly e-newsletter that people subscribe to on my Web site. When I send out a bit of inspiration two to four times each month, it reaches thousands of individuals. I carefully consider the messages I send because I recognize their ability to influence people's decisions and perspectives. People often respond to tell me I wrote just what they needed to hear that week, so I take this opportunity very seriously!

Whether you are a hairstylist, a stay-at-home parent, a bus driver, or a doctor, you have a sphere of influence that grows as you succeed. Be open to the ways you can impact those who cross your path and ways you can connect people together for greater purposes.

4. *At this stage of my life, what is my divine assignment?* Each of us has a unique mission in life. That mission can be reflected in a variety of ways. For example, a man whose purpose, or mission, is to help others reach their highest potential may at different times serve as a mentor to a troubled teenager, an art teacher, a life coach, or any of a number of other roles. I call these changing tasks "divine assignments" because God has given each of us unique talents and passions and has directed us toward various situations and certain people for a purpose. But the ways we fulfill that purpose will evolve over time. As we grow and experience success and failure, our divine assignments change. Fulfilling a given assignment doesn't mean you've fully achieved your purpose; it means it's time to move on to a new

assignment. Review the experiences that have shaped your personal and professional growth during the past few years, and let them lead you toward a new divine assignment that you alone are uniquely capable of completing.

Asking "What's next?" can be invigorating or intimidating, depending on your attitude. But remaining stuck at the finish line of your last victory won't help you become the person God created you to be. Take time now to search the horizon for the new dreams that will determine your next steps.

Closing the Gap

Focus Your Thoughts
Spend some time alone in a quiet place, allowing yourself to contemplate whatever comes to mind when you ask yourself, "What are my unfulfilled dreams?" Imagine your life as you'd like it to be. Dream big.

Use Your Words Wisely
Write down everything that came to mind when you asked the previous question. Describe in vivid detail your life as you envision it five, ten, and twenty years from now.

Target Your Actions
Choose one of the dreams you identified above, and write out an action plan for making it a reality. Then take the first step this week.

Energize Your Spirit

Lord, I'm listening for Your direction because I know that when You order my steps, my future is sure. Prod me when I'm tempted to rest on past accomplishments, and keep me mindful of Your purpose for my life. Open my eyes to the opportunities that lie ahead. Amen.

Thirty-Four

What Do You Need to Leave Behind?

Let Go of Whatever Is Weighing You Down

Tina approached me after one of my speaking engagements. She found her profession less than fulfilling and wanted to transition into another line of work, but she worried that the idea of a career change at her age was ridiculous. "I feel like I can't just go changing careers at thirty-two," she said. "I've set my course, and it seems like it's just too late to change my mind."

Tina's comments reflect a common misperception. So much emphasis is placed on choosing what career to pursue—especially during the high-school and college years—that it seems such a decision must be permanent. But interests evolve, needs change, and any of us should be free to move in a new direction. Tina needed to change her attitudes and beliefs just as much as she needed to change her career.

When you feel led in a new direction yet resist turning onto a new path, your soul will feel misplaced. And even when you do summon the courage to follow a new trail, you'll find yourself stumbling along the way unless you trade your old provisions for equipment suited to your new challenges. Certain things that served you well at an earlier point in your journey may not complement your current goals and priorities. If you don't let go of these aspects of your life, they'll weigh you down like so much excess baggage, hindering your attempts to move forward.

Sarah, for example, had outgrown a particular group of friends. Their obsession with celebrity gossip, the latest fashions, and impressing others no longer fit her values. As she grew spiritually and felt compelled to share her exciting new goals, her friends didn't show the least bit of interest. In fact, they treated her like a bit of an oddball. She constantly found herself battling doubt, feeling defensive, and trying to explain herself. The problem lay not in Tina or even necessarily in her friends but in the huge gap between their priorities and hers. She had begun a deeper walk of faith and needed friends who could support her and accompany her on that journey. Finally she decided to become more active in her church and join a ministry with members whose interests and values reflected her own. Her decision opened the doorway to new friendships that helped her move forward on her spiritual journey.

As you follow your unique path and move toward the best that your life has to offer, you'll encounter new situations that require you to leave behind the familiar and step out in faith to embrace the unfamiliar. It can be tempting to hold on to a job, relationship, attitude, possession, or even old ways of thinking for far too long. Those things then become weights that leave you unable to take advantage of the opportunities before you. If you are unwilling to let go of "what was" in order to embrace "what can be," you'll miss out on the experiences that will help you grow, succeed, and maximize your success.

Some things in life you can only attain by letting go of the old and making room for something better. The process reminds me of one of my favorite spots on the playground as a child—the monkey bars. In order to swing from one bar to the next, you must for a brief moment let go of one bar so that you can reach for the next. It's unsettling, but if you don't let go as you reach for the next bar, you'll find yourself dangling by one arm, having lost all momentum. The same is true for our attempts to close the gaps in our lives. Sometimes success can be found only by letting go.

If you refuse to let go at the appropriate time, God will sometimes wrench out of your grasp whatever it is you're clinging to so that you'll be free to move forward. At the time such changes may not seem positive or helpful. In fact, you may feel hurt, frustrated, and frightened when familiar circumstances come to an end. But trust that God has a plan. He is doing it to lighten your load and prepare you for the next stage in life.

At age twenty-four, I had the unique opportunity to start my own business. Staying with my full-time job certainly would have been the safer choice: I had a guaranteed paycheck and a set routine of projects. Although I'd held the position less than two years, it felt familiar and I truly loved the people and the family atmosphere. But I'd had a strong entrepreneurial spirit since childhood, and I'd set a goal of launching a business by the age of thirty. So when other companies began asking for my help with their marketing efforts, I couldn't resist the chance to strike out on my own— even though the opportunity was coming six years earlier planned. Letting go of the safety of employment to reach for the dream of business ownership meant seizing the moment. Starting the business with clients provided momentum that I didn't want to lose. More important, God's prompting gave me the confidence to believe I could succeed. So I decided to make the change. It was a lot of hard work and I really missed the comraderie of being a part of a bigger company, but I made a decision to never look back. No one could have adequately described for me ahead of time the challenges or the sheer gratification I would face as the creator of my own business. The experience grew me quickly and immensely. And it provided a platform for writing and promoting my first book—an achievement that, most likely, I otherwise would not have attained in my twenties. Letting go of the comfortable and reaching for the uncomfortable was a critical step in my journey.

One of my favorite scriptures is Philippians 3:13, in which the apostle Paul wrote, "One thing I do, forgetting those things which are behind and reaching forward to those things which are ahead."

What do you need to leave behind so that you can reach forward to what is ahead in your life?

Closing the Gap

Focus Your Thoughts
Meditate on the words of the apostle Paul in Philippians 3:13-14: "One thing I do, forgetting those things which are behind and reaching forward to those things which are ahead, I press toward the goal for the prize of the upward call of God in Christ Jesus."

Use Your Words Wisely
In your journal write out your answer to these questions: "What am I afraid to let go of?" "Why?"

Target Your Actions

Based on your answer to the previous questions, develop a plan of action to lighten your load by letting go of any circumstance, relationship, idea, or anything else that is weighing you down.

Energize Your Spirit

Lord, help me let go of things that no longer fit Your purpose for my life. I trust You to provide what I need and to take from me any burdens that hinder me from breaking through to my best life. Amen.

Thirty-Five

How Far Have You Come?

Draw Strength and Hope from Your Positive Progress

When you're not moving forward as quickly as you might like, it's easy to get discouraged. But as long as you refuse to remain stuck—choosing instead to confront your fears and issues—you are making progress. If you take baby steps to complete a hundred-yard dash, it may take you a lot longer than Marion Jones to make it to the finish line, but you'll get there!

Giving birth to a dream, like giving birth to a child, is a process that involves joy mingled with pain. Periods of energetic activity are interspersed with moments of fear, doubt, and exhaustion. The closer you are to seeing your dream become reality, the more discomfort you'll most likely experience. You may be tempted to give up, to wonder if the outcome will be worth the effort. Let me assure you that it will.

Often, just as you believe you are nearing a breakthrough, you may enter a period of turmoil in your business, relationships, or finances, or in another area of your life. Sadly, this is when many people choose to give up. Rather than concluding that the price is too high or the journey is too long, keep pushing forward. This is the time to remind yourself of your ultimate goals and to dig deep for the determination you will need to achieve them.

Many motivated, ambitious people are so focused on the tasks ahead that they forget to celebrate the progress they've already made. You may feel that you're miles from where you would like to be, but I'm certain you've made progress in many areas of your life. Just by working through this book, you've taken a huge step forward. Give yourself credit for the strength and tenacity it has taken for you to make it this far, and draw strength from how far you've come.

We all have different starting points in life, and we need to evaluate our progress based on individual circumstances, not on the standards set by others. For example, a person who grew up in an abusive and dysfunctional household should acknowledge the effort it has taken him to nurture a successful, stable marriage and peaceful family life. The entrepreneur who has built a successful business out of nothing should acknowledge the accomplishment and allow it to reenergize her hope when times are difficult.

When you ask yourself, "How far have I come?" you do several important things:

1. *You validate your efforts and progress.* When a new door opens as a result of your vigorous pursuit of an opportunity, it's important to pause long enough to acknowledge your efforts before dashing on. Recognize what you've just accomplished and reward yourself for hard work.

2. *You resist comparing yourself with others.* Because we don't start from the same point, it's unfair to compare our current circumstances with those of others. Each of us has been given a different set of skills and talents and has been blessed with unique experiences. Deliberately choosing to acknowledge your progress helps you remain focused on the destination to which God is leading you rather than wishing you were on someone else's path.

3. *You acknowledge the courage you've shown.* Making progress in our lives requires us to stand up for ourselves, do things we may not particularly enjoy, and overcome fears, obstacles, and misperceptions. When you reflect on how far you've come, you'll recognize the strength of character you've developed—character you'll need as you persevere through the process of birthing your dream.

4. *You notice what your life is teaching you.* Everything we experience in life holds a lesson, if we are paying attention. By pausing to examine what you've learned, you'll be better prepared to recognize new opportunities for growth and fulfillment.

5. *You notice who you are becoming on your journey.* If you are growing at all, you are not the same person today that you were a year ago or five years ago. Asking "How far have I come?" allows you to reflect on your own personal transformation into a wiser, stronger, and more spiritually mature person.

Take a moment today to look back on your progress in your relationships, career, finances and resources, physical health and environments, and spiritual life. Appreciating how far you've come just may provide the energy you need to keep pressing on and take the steps to close the gap between where you are and where you want to be.

Closing the Gap

Focus Your Thoughts

Meditate on these words: "And let us not grow weary while doing good, for in due season we shall reap if we do not lose heart" (Galatians 6:9).

Use Your Words Wisely

Rather than complaining, "I'm exhausted. I'm tired of working so hard," ask yourself, "The journey is tiring at times. How can I renew my strength?"

Target Your Actions

Take a moment today to answer this question, "Given my starting point, how did I make it as far as I am now?" Perhaps you can credit your courage, perseverance, ingenuity, hard work, or some other quality. Acknowledge your progress, pat yourself on the back, and keep pushing ahead!

Energize Your Spirit

God, please grant me the endurance to persevere and the wisdom to learn important lessons along my journey. Place in me the desire to push ahead with excellence, even when I am weary. Amen.

Are You Ready to Close the Gap?

Choose to Move Forward in Faith

I believe that nothing in life is a coincidence and that this book made it into your hands for a reason. So what are you going to do now? My prayer is that working through these pages has not only helped you identify what's really holding you back but has also enabled you to chart a course that will close the gap between where you are and where you want to be.

We are each responsible to understand ourselves and to become aware of how our experiences have shaped us and contribute to our innermost fears. Out of that awareness, we can gain the insight and wisdom to overcome the most persistent issues in our lives.

Life is a precious gift, and we need to live it to the fullest. You don't want to look back over your life knowing that so much more was possible if only you had been willing to face your fears and work through your issues. You don't have to live in bondage to fears, obstacles, and misperceptions. God wants you to be free to live the life He created you to live.

Just as important, God wants you to stay on the path He created for you—even when the going is rough, even when you feel like running in the other direction. God knows what you have been through. He knows what you are afraid of. He knows your weaknesses. And He still believes in your potential.

To reach for that potential, you must take authority over your thoughts, use your words as weapons of positive power, take steps forward despite your fears, and energize your spirit through constant prayer and meditation.

You do not have to be held back any longer. The sooner you choose to move forward, the sooner you can begin to realize your best possible life. Remember these keys as you seek to close the gaps in your life:

- *Be driven by pure motives.* To fully realize your potential, you need to be sure the fuel that drives you forward is pure. The underlying purpose of your vision is to serve God, use your talents and experiences, and make a difference in the world on His behalf. Refuse to allow your negative emotions, ego, insecurities, or selfishness to be the driving force behind your vision.

- *Pray for wisdom.* Understanding your issues and fears—and overcoming them—requires spiritual maturity and wisdom. Seek the divine wisdom you need to understand yourself, your emotions, and your self-sabotaging habits.

- *Listen to the messages your emotions are sending.* Do not ignore emotions or allow your reactions to become so automatic that you don't even notice the messages they're sending. Instead, let your feelings inform you of the issues that need to be explored so that they don't restrain you from making progress.

- *Take action, learn, and adjust.* At each step along the way, notice what you have learned from the actions you've taken. Then adjust your course based upon that knowledge. Take a new and improved action; then learn from it and adjust your course once more. Growth occurs through this cycle of action and learning—and growth is what the journey is all about.

Although this book is coming to a close, I invite you to continue to use it as a personal resource. If you know others who are held back from achieving their true potential, give them a copy of the book. Together you can encourage and even coach one another on your individual journeys.

Remember, your transformation is a process. Some gaps will be harder to close than others. Don't give up. Persist with patience, trusting that God has perfect timing.

And enjoy the freedom you've gained by identifying and conquering the issues that have held you back!

For a reader's guide suitable for individual or group use,
please visit www.ValorieBurton.com.
